Coffee Saved My Life

A Memoir

By Lindsey Buboltz

Praise for Coffee Saved My Life

"I lived through most of these stories with Lindsey and still couldn't put the book down. She has always been my anchor through life and after reading these stories I realize she has also been my shield. She protected me from feeling her pain, only showed me the good parts and always 'had my back.'"

Melissa Rosander

"She's amazing. I've seen her go through everything- she comes out stronger. She loves others and loves to watch others succeed (not just financial, but in their lives). She makes other realize their greatness."

Ryan Buboltz

"...her tough exterior is a cover for a huge and giving heart. I am blessed to have been able to watch my friend evolve into a wonderful giving leader and a successful businesswoman."

Melissa Johnson

Coffee
Saved My Life

A MEMOIR

Lindsey Buboltz

Pierucci Publishing 2021

Copyright

Cataloguing in publication information is
Available from Library and Archives U.S.
ISBN 978-0-578-93863-9 (paperback)

Pierucci Publishing
www.Pieruccipublishing.com

Cover design by Stephanie Pierucci at Pierucci Publishing
Printed and Bound by Corporate Disk Fulfillment

LindseyBuboltz.com
#littlecoffeebiz
#coffeesavedmylife

Disclaimer

This book is meant to narrate one woman's subjective journey while learning about how to use the power of her mind for a happy and healthy life. The information provided by the author, website, or this company is not a substitute for a face-to-face consultation with your physician and should not be construed as individual medical advice. If a condition persists, please contact your physician. This book is provided for personal and informational purposes only. This book is not to be construed as any attempt to either prescribe or practice medicine. Neither is the site to be understood as putting forth any cure for any type of acute or chronic health problem. You should always consult with a competent, fully licensed medical professional when making any decision regarding your health. The owners of **lindseybuboltz.com** will use reasonable efforts to include up-to-date and accurate information on our Internet site, but make no representations, warranties, or assurances as to the accuracy, currency, or completeness of the information provided. The owners of this book and our corresponding internet site shall not be liable for any damages or injury resulting from your access to, or inability to access this book, our Internet site, or from your reliance upon any information provided. All rights reserved. No part of this publication may be reproduced, transmitted, transcribed, stored in a retrieval system, or translated into any language, in any form, by any means, without the written permission of the author.

Lindsey Buboltz
Little Coffee Biz, LLC
www.LindseyBuboltz.com

Dedication

To my husband Ryan, for showing me what true love really
is, for supporting me in writing this book
and always encouraging me to dream bigger!
I love you baby!

Table of Contents

Foreword

"Change your thoughts and you can change your world."
- Norman Vincent Peale

Lindsey Buboltz is the epitome of perseverance and optimism, impacting the lives of thousands of people, soon to be millions. From pain to purpose and beyond.

Her experiences shared in Coffee Saved My Life reminds you that it is not your situation that is holding you back. It's the way you approach it. I recommend this book to anyone needing inspiration and an adjustment to their mindset to start.

I encourage you to read this book very deliberately. It will take you through years of trauma, trials and tribulation while providing hope, inspiration and much-needed healing. After reading and digesting this life-changing book, you will have your eyes opened to the healing capacity that you have within you. I read this book very carefully, taking notes as I went along, mostly because I have so much respect for the woman who created it. I can say with certainty that the contents of this powerful book have brought me to tears and a whole new awareness and level of compassion.

I love this book, and I love the woman who created it. Thank you, Lindsey - Coffee Saved My Life is destined to become a best seller, and I am honored that you asked me to write the Foreword for it.

P.S. As you read along, mark the pages that resonate with you. You'll want to refer back to them on the days when you're feeling brokenhearted, destitute or beat down.

Share this book with family and friends.

Give a copy to someone who needs a boost. And, when you need a reminder that life is filled with blessings, opportunities, joy, overcoming, surviving, and thriving return to this book. You'll find just what you need to keep on keeping on, looking ahead with gratitude while recognizing all the good in your life now - and to come.

-Babette Teno, BS, CN, CGP, CLE
Nutritionist, Speaker, Publicist, Author, Coach
Co-Founder, Sisters on Stages - "Speaker Bookings, Coaching, Public Relations, Media & More"

Warning

The stories you're about to read may make you laugh... but they'll make you cry much more.

I haven't had an easy life, and you're about to read about it.

What I want you to know is that there IS a happy ending to my story... and to yours.

If you're feeling lost, dismayed, or otherwise disenchanted with life...

Please visit me at www.LindseyBuboltz.com where you can get your hands on this magical coffee, or just scan this code with your phone.

Love,

Lindsey
June, 2021

Prologue

I wasn't dealt the best hand at life. At times it's felt like I've experienced seven or eight lifetimes of pain. Maybe twenty. All packed into this one life.

My parents sucked. I was sexually abused. I've been cheated on more times than I can count. I've had men leave in the middle of the night. I've had men beat me. I have had men beat my children. Parents have left me for other families. People I loved have killed themselves. And, one Mother's Day night, my daughter was murdered.

Depression and anxiety were once constant and unrelenting companions.

My life has been hard. Difficult. Excruciating at times. For many years it seemed like every time things finally seemed to be going okay, the bottom would fall out again. Just fall out, and I would sink—sink into stuffing myself with food, sink into stuffing myself with Xanax, sink into not getting out of bed for days on end, sink into hospitalizing panic attacks.

But I've always gotten up. Because I've never given up. I never gave into all of those suicidal thoughts, the ones that started way back when I was fourteen. And here I am, today, happy. Fulfilled. Moving forward. Living my dream life.

I've found hope. I've found purpose. I've found meaning. Through helping others.

*

And my hope is, now, that with this book—through telling my story—*you* can find hope. That, yeah, though it can be full of pain, life can also be beautiful. That life can actually be *good*.

My hope, dear reader, is that this book inspires you to take on whatever obstacles are in your way—be them external or internal—and overcome them.

My hope, what keeps me going, is that I can help people. And with this book, I hope to help you.

My hope is to show you that it doesn't matter where you've been—it only matters where you are going.

—Lindsey

Chapter I

Childhood

I know you're supposed to 'disconnect from your mind' and all that, but my mind is where I get my best thoughts.

Sometimes, though, my mind plays with me. Like some old-time horror film reel. Like when it plays my very first memory of life. The one of me in the backseat of my mom's '77 Chevy Nova. On one of the rides where we're going to the penitentiary to see my dad. For some reason, my mind keeps playing it. Thirty-seven years later and the horror film is still going—my mom up front in the Nova on that cold, grey day on what must've been Interstate 80 from Omaha to Lincoln to the Nebraska State Penitentiary.

I see my mom's hands on the steering wheel. Just her hands. Nothing else mattered. I see her hands shifting nervously back and forth on the wheel. They are not calm. She was not calm. The car was filled with the energy of what I would later learn to be called fear—my first memory. My first memory is fear.

The memory continues as we park, walk cautiously inside, and are greeted with pat downs, just trying to see my dad, and we have to be completely checked over just to get inside the penitentiary. All these stranger's hands on me and my mom. Men with guns. Fear. And then I see my dad, I see him in all-tan clothing hobbling out to see us. And there are all these rules.

I don't understand any of it, you know, what was going on. I was two-and-a-half. I was afraid.
My mind makes me relive that first memory all the time. To this day.

Then that mind of mine will move on, and I'll go about my day for a bit. Get some work done. Have a cup of coffee. A little reprieve from the horror film. But not long.

What'll come up on the marquee next? Yep. That first sexual assault at five. I remember everything about it. My brother. That look in his eyes. The fear in mine. The icky feeling. The tears.

Oh, and here's this one: dad coming home from prison, it's clouded but it's there, the forced smiles and laughter. We were supposed to be happy. I don't think I was. I was afraid.

Next horror film up—and this one's crystal clear. My mind plays this one a lot, the night my dad assaulted my mom. His fists. Her blood. One moment we were watching *The Honeymooners* and the next I just wanted to disappear. I remember that night like it was yesterday. What I saw through my child's eyes: The blood pouring from her head as she lay on the floor. The growl of his words as he towers above her: "Shut up or I'll do it again!"

Then the memory reel gives me images of us packing all our stuff into big black garbage bags and loading up the car and disappearing in the middle of a day to go to a safe house. It is awful. It is fear.

I do remember Shirley, the woman with the grin at the safe house who gave me candy and toys—the one half-smile my memory gives me. One half-smile in the ocean of fear. That's all I have.
And that's really all I remember from my early life. All I remember from being a little girl. Seems weird, right?

I think it's that mind-thing again. Playing with me. See, it's taken away all the other details from early childhood, every memory—maybe in some effort to save me from them. I don't know.

16

Those first few years exist in my mind only as a few memories, a few images amid some chaotic and fear-filled blur from where I sprung into becoming who I am today.

Chapter II

Up and then Down Again

I was three years old, and fear remained a constant companion. Then Jeff became my mom's new 'true love.' He was the first great thing in my life.

Jeff was the first person, my memories tell me, to ever believe in me. He showed up into my life, and he believed in me. He was the first person to show up to my softball games and cheer me on. The first person I could cry to. He'd hear me sobbing upstairs in my room and show up with a box of Kleenex. He'd give me a tissue and listen to me. He made me feel safe. Like I was protected. He was the first adult that didn't hurt me. He always took care of me. Until he couldn't.

Jeff was a truck driver, a good one and everyone liked him. So he ended up getting more routes, more gigs. Was out on the road more often and for longer at a time. I missed him.

So did my mom. She'd finally found something good and didn't want to lose it. She made the decision to leave me and go out on the road with him. She chose Jeff over me.

I would have too.

I was forced to go live with my father—that guy from the penitentiary. Not too long after getting out, he'd left us and gone and started a whole new family. I guess he couldn't stand my mom either. And now that Jeff and mom were living out on the road, I was sent to live with him. Him and his new family.

A lot was different, but a lot stayed the same. The sexual assault continued—my brother had come with me to live with our dad. And night after night, he'd show up in my room with that look in his eye.

"No!" I'd say.

"Shut up," he'd say, and then he'd go at it.

Night after night.

I was living life full of a rage that I didn't know what to call. It was pervasive. It was all around. It was inside me. The rage *was* me.

*

One day I was outside my house on the sidewalk, and this little neighbor girl—I don't even recall what she did to put me over the edge—but I know that I picked up a handful of dirt and I threw it, hard, right into her face.

My siblings ran inside. "Don't tell dad on me!" I yelled to them.

But that's exactly what they did. And that night was the first time I experienced a beating so bad it made the simple act of sitting down unbearable.

But I still had to go to school. Third grade. And my teacher saw me grimace as I took my chair. She asked me a few questions and sent me to the counselor's office where I shared my story of the dirt throwing and my dad's punishment.

"You can tell us," they said. "It's only between you and us. It's private. No one's going to know."

But they lied. I told them the details, and they sent the state in and removed my brothers and sisters from the care of my dad's family. And it wasn't like how you'd envision child protective services doing their job, wasn't nice, wasn't calm. They literally made my dad pack our bags in ten minutes and drop us off on the doorstep of Children's Square, a group home for kids like me—for kids without families.

Again, I don't remember much about this time. Just a few images in that horror film. They didn't have my favorite cereal. I remember that. And I remember this: when my dad dropped us off on that first that day, I had a Walmart bag full of my clothes and toys. I was told to leave them in the truck, told that we "have everything you need. That bag, little girl, stays with your father."

So it did. My life stayed. And I went to live in a group home.

We were taken into this big room full of fold-out tables stacked with clothes. It looked like a garage sale with all the pants and shirts and sweaters sorted by size, and we were told that we could pick two outfits.

But nothing matched.

"Nothing matches!" I screamed with my nine-year-old vocal cords. "These clothes suck!"

My new life sucked. My life sucked. Even as a kid, a child, I knew this truth.

Chapter III

Children's Square

Shortly into my stay at Children's Square, I am eight years old and I remember one night waking to my brother, screaming. I woke to him screaming wildly at one of his friends he'd caught assaulting my sister. Sexually.

"Stop that!" my brother yelled at him. He ran over and punched him and pushed him away from my sister.

I didn't understand. Why was he so upset—he did the same things to me? I didn't understand. He came in like a hero to protect my sister from the same pain he caused me, and I hated him for it.

"How can he not see this?" I asked God that night.

That was the day that I understood all this was wrong, that what was happening to me at the hands of my brother and other males in my life was not okay. Because at that point I don't think I had realized, "this isn't normal. This isn't what is supposed to be happening to me."

I finally saw it. It was really the first awakening of my life. I've had a few, but that first one took a long time to click.

*

We were at the Children's Square group home for an indeterminate amount of my mind's chaotic horror-film memory-blur—and then mom appeared from off the road.

"Where has she been?" I asked my sister.

We never found out exactly. She had just been gone, out on the road. We left that day with her. But Jeff was back! He bought us a trailer in the trailer park, you know, a 'good' home. At least I could pick out my own cereal. Lucky Charms. Especially the marshmallows.

And Jeff bought me clothes that matched.

Life felt almost normal, whatever that word is supposed to mean. The rage inside quieted a little bit. It was a time of less fear.

Mom even stopped the drinking. Gave it up and went dry. She'd been bad with booze my whole life and probably most of hers. Getting sober made her more giving, and she tried hard to amend for prior sins.

She had a lot of them to amend for.

Chapter IV

We Won! (Sort of)

So here we are, like life's kind of 'normal.' Less fear. My brother wasn't showing up in my bedroom at night. I even got to go swimming in the pool. And then my stepdad, that awesome man named Jeff? He won. He won a half a million dollars. From a $5 scratch-off.

Yeah, that happened. It was awesome.

We were out of the trailer park and had become the owners of one of the largest pieces of property in Guthrie Center, Iowa.

It was a few miles out of town on Poplar Avenue, passed the S-turns and all the trees. The house was white with green trim and green shutters. A big living room and kitchen and two bedrooms downstairs with more rooms up above. There was a big circle driveway and over 300 acres of pasture grounds in which we could play. There was even a spring, and we used to love drinking that ice-cold water. It was something fresh, something pure, and I loved that water. And there was this big rock, a boulder out on the property where we'd drive the four-wheelers to sunbathe. My sister Carrie and I would sunbathe and talk about boys and look at the horizon and the clouds. It was a fresh start.

We showed up in this tiny little farm town and of course everybody knew we were the family that just won the lottery and had moved on in. I don't know what they said down at the café when we weren't around, but for me it was cool—like being the talk of the town or something. It was summer. Late in the summer before I started seventh grade. It seemed like everybody knew our business. Some boys even knew my name. We moved to Guthrie Center, and it was like a fresh start.

It was like, I'm going to get to relax, rewrite my life story at this point. And things got off to a really amazing start; I met my first childhood best friends: Nicole and Melissa.

Though it was Jeff's nickel that scratched across the golden ticket to illuminate the prize, for a little over one year it felt like *I* had won the lottery.

*

Then came high school.

Over the course of a couple years, my mom and Jeff's relationship had dissolved. Things weren't working. Jeff was this charismatic guy, and everyone loved him. Including, I guess, other women. He had an affair. At least one.

"Jeff's moving out," my mother told me one night.

There were a couple more arguments between them, the harsh words and the cold silences, and then he sold the house. Then he left. Then I never heard from him again. Ever. The man who'd really been the only dad figure in my life. My father. My strength. Everything that held me up. Gone. In a flash.

I learned to know that whenever things were going good in my life, that was just about when the bottom would fall out.

We found a house in town and the family, minus Jeff, we all moved in. I missed the Poplar house both instantly and immensely. Things were different. Not as good. A dip in the rollercoaster. A flash of the horror film. I had to move on.

I had to find a way to just push through. It wasn't easy but in time I found a way. I don't know whether it was healthy, but this is what I did: I channeled all the hurt and all the anger into a sort of tenacity and grit to prove him wrong. To prove that Jeff should have stayed because "I'm so good, and Goodbye Jeff! I don't need you! ... but, come back?"

I made the varsity volleyball team as a sophomore. I worked my butt off and made the team. I was the only sophomore to make it. I thought that would impress him enough to have him show up in the stands like he used to for my softball games and youth track meets. But he didn't come. Never came to see me make one dig or set or spike. Not once. More hurt and anger was boiling inside of me. Even at a young age, I somehow knew to turn it into tenacity and grit.

I threw myself into being an athlete, an athlete and a straight-A student. The more I put into being an athlete, the less I had to be at home. Which was a good thing. Plus, my volleyball coach, Coach Cole, believed in me. He saw something in me, and I could feel it. I'd get to school early, stay late after practice. To spend more around Coach Cole and to not have to be 'at home.' I was doing good in high school.

But even in this seemingly personal endeavor, I had to overcome my two older siblings. They were always in my way. If it wasn't sexual assault, it was verbal assault.

My brother and sister gone through this same high school a few years before me. The teachers remembered them. They remembered my longhaired, hard-fighting, class-failing brother. The guy always on the verge of dropping out or failing out just biding his time before the drugs really start to take control.

Then there was my sister. My sister was 'the skinny one,' (and she never let me forget that) the super pretty one that all the boys want to date and the girls want to be around. And she was always out, always "going out!" with her friends to concerts and parties and spending the night at boys' houses.

But then the drugs got her too. First it was too much booze. Then pot. Then, well then, it was the meth.

So anyway, neither were good students. They were the type of kid a teacher remembers. Last names. Facial profile for future potential progeny walking through the halls or, God forbid, ever coming to take a seat in their classroom.

I had to prove myself. I'd had some experience in doing this. Was getting good at this. So I did it. Proved that I wasn't like my kin. That I was different, better. I worked hard and overcame the prejudice my siblings had earned for me. After midterms of the first semester, I'm sitting in Health Class—lots of picture-diagram posters on the wall and Doc Litter with his odd mannerisms—and he's walking the rows of desks as he passed back the exams.

He slapped mine down on the table face down and looked at me in the eye. "I would have never expected this from a Cullinane," he said, and he turned over the paper to reveal a 97%.

I remember him saying that to me: "I never expected this from a Cullinane." And instead of hearing his words for what he probably intended them to be, I heard "you're a failure, just like the rest of them." But I knew I was different. I would not be like them.

I started to exert control, over anything and everything I could. I needed to feel 'in control' of my life, so I sought to control every little last detail—over every class, every test, every friendship, every relationship. Throughout my whole life I had watched my dad walk all over my stepmom, and Jeff, as good as he was for a time to me, walked away from my mom. My brother had repeatedly taken advantage of me sexually, psychologically, as a bully.

I had another great awakening: "I am taking control of my life," I told myself.

Trouble is, I was a fourteen-year-old girl who had no idea how to do that. I tried to exert agency where and how I could (three suspensions in three years), power, and it turned into fighting at school which turned into suspensions. Which turned into being kicked off of the volleyball team. Which turned into my friend's parents saying, "you know, I don't want that Lindsey girl at our sleepovers. I don't want you hanging out with that girl."

The shunning played straight into my mental state. Badly. I put up a wall, a real 'fuck you' attitude, and things got rough. I got rough. My life got even rougher.

"No, fuck *you*—I'm gonna do what *I* want," became my motto, my mantra, my shield. And so I did. I wanted to take control of my own destiny, and in my pubescent mind that meant flouting the system and partying. If I couldn't have happiness, at least maybe I could have some fun.

By fifteen, I was running through the cornfield fields and hiding in the hay bales to escape the cops. There were boys to kiss. Girls to kiss. Vodka to be chugged. I had gotten in with a new crowd (usually a cautionary tale, and it was for me) and we were having the time of our lives. I was partying it up, numbing it out—my mind, the horror-film reel, that is.

*

To pay for the booze and all my shenanigans, I got my first job. One of the 'head cashiers' at the grocery store in town. This was actually a good thing. A little victory among the sea of defeats. I got to see new people, meet new people. Crazy as it seems, it put me 'on stage' a little bit: Me behind the register asking how a person's day was going as I rang up for groceries. I got to make people smile, got to get a taste of what being a positive light for someone else can feel like—simply by just showing up and ringing up their groceries with a smile and wishing them a good day. Yep. And there is something in these memories that tells me I was starting the stages of my recovery from all the trauma.

But then, of course, more trauma was just around the corner. That was the pattern for me.

Chapter V

The Adult Teenager

Mom got a new boyfriend. My life was always changing based on "mom's new man." The summer before my junior year, the boyfriend was moving to Omaha. Mom couldn't bear not going with him. That meant me too. Back to Omaha. My sister and brother were done with high school, and so it would just be me.

"I'm not going back to Omaha," I told my mom, the words dripping with the teenage angst I had worked so hard to cultivate. "I finally found my home—I'm finishing school *here*."

I took it upon myself to exert control over my own life. That's probably the biggest (only?) thing I learned growing up. To depend on myself because no one else was there for me.

Mom had gone to Omaha with her new man. She was gone, and I had stayed. On my own. I got through the suspensions at school and got back to work. My GPA had dropped, but I had got it back up to a 3.6. I had a car. I met a boy. Well, a young man. His name was Rory.

Rory was a few years older than my sixteen, for sure illegal by today's statutory rule. But, hey, I loved him, and he at least showed that he liked me. Supposedly he'd had a crush on me for a few years, and for whatever reason we finally ended up together. And so here I have this relationship and this life and I'm working and I'm putting myself through high school, and things are going well. But, for me, when things were going good was just when the bottom was about to fall out.

*

Mom left and Rory and I found an abandoned house in the middle of town to 'live' in—no water, no electricity, no heat. The kitchen wasn't functional. There was literally one decent room that we threw an air mattress in.

At least it had a roof and four walls.

We squatted there for a while like hobos. In my naivete, I didn't see how wrong it was. I didn't see how wrong it was that I didn't expect *more*. I didn't see how wrong it was to accept what 'was.'

Then this happened: I found out Rory was expecting a child—with someone else. He'd apparently knocked someone up when we'd broken up for a couple weeks.

"Fuck you!" came my standard retort. I was crushed. Yeah, friends had warned me about him, and people did say it was a little odd how much older he was than me, me being just a little sweet sixteen 'n all.

I pushed all the advice to the side and took 'control.' I loved this person. "We were destined to be together," my young mind told me. I wasn't going to let this pregnancy ruin it.

I'm sixteen. I'm working full-time. I'm getting good marks in school. I'm having fun. I have a boyfriend. Things aren't perfect but I worked hard at Life.

I must have pushed too hard. I became ill, sick, downcast, and I couldn't go to school.
I called the school. "Uh, yeah. . . I'm sick and won't be in today."

No dice—a minor requires a note from a parent to be excused from school. I didn't have any parents. My *parents* were absent.

School caught wind of this. They heard about my living situation in the abandoned house. It was "not tolerable." I was sick as hell and feeling awful. There seemed to be no hope.

But then the ying-yang of life kicked it. My best friend Nicole's parents, Peggy and Otis, stepped up and offered to take over guardianship of me. They drove over one day and took a look at my living situation and told me I could come live with them. They wrote my notes for school to get my absences covered and offered me a real home. It helped. It really did.

I moved in with them and, for a short time, I had a family. But it wasn't meant to last. I was sixteen and I didn't like having people telling me what I could and couldn't do. I was all about control, right? Like a good teenager, I knew 'everything' and was going to conquer the world on my own. I had to move out. Rory and I broke up, and I needed to spread my wings. I needed to be on my own.

I went to the little motel in town that'd been converted to one of those 'extended stay apartment' type things, and I strode up to the owner of the place, a kind old woman named Pat, and begged for an apartment of my own. But I was just sixteen and didn't have any legal rights to rent an apartment.

"Why should I rent you this apartment?" she asked.

"Because I need it," I said, and she must have seen the look of determination in my eyes.
She said, "okay then," and she rented me a unit.

Sixteen and feeling as free and independent as a country song. I was on my own. I was paying my own bills. I was living in *my* apartment. No matter it was about the tiniest little studio apartment you could ever imagine, it was mine. Four walls and a roof with a sink and a toilet and a shower that worked. Even a little kitchenette. And no one could take it from me.

And then Shakiah was born. I didn't give birth to her, but right away she felt like she was mine. We had an instant connection and I loved her from the first moment I saw her. She was perfect.

Fast forward a few months. I'm a senior in high school and Rory and I are back together. We're living together in my apartment and we're raising Shakiah together. I have some control over my life.

Until I did the laundry one day.

I'm doing laundry and I'm washing one of Rory's work shirts. I see something in the chest pocket. It's a note, a note with another girl's handwriting: digits, a phone number.

I picked up the phone and called the number. "How do you know Rory?" I demanded.

"Ah, who are *you*? Rory's my boyfriend."

Yep. That's what she said. Her name ended up being Ashley. Rory had played me good.

That night I told him to move out. We fought and went to sleep. He must have woken up and packed his bags because when I got up in the morning he was gone. All his clothes and belongings were gone. He was gone. But his baby still lay in her cradle next to me. Shakiah. Shakiah and me. Like it would be for years.

I raised her as my own. Even though I knew she could be taken from me at any time, I raised her like my daughter. Because she was. It was life. It was my life. I lived it—*we* lived it, together.

Now you can be Free! Rest in Paradise baby girl!

*

In school, all that anger and fear had turned to tenacity and grit, and I ended up graduating high school early, with honors. I graduated in December, six months earlier than the kids who had life handed to them with silver spoons, all while working and raising a baby without the help of a mom or a dad. I did it. I had to.

I ended up filing for legal emancipation from my parents to guarantee financial aid for college. I wanted to chase my dreams, and free tuition seemed like a good avenue. I got a financial aid scholarship, nearly a full ride, to

Midland University (Midland Lutheran College as it was known then). I was going to become a social worker. I was going to go change the lives of other kids who were dealt hands like mine—so they would never have to fold.

I knew I couldn't bring a baby into the dorms, but I didn't know if I could afford my own apartment again. Omaha was more expensive than Guthrie Center. I looked into every angle. I contacted attorneys. I thought about stripping. Would have. But then the law told me I had "no rights to Shakiah." I cried every tear I had. I fought with my mind all night long. In the morning, I made the hardest phone call of my life. I called Rory's grandmother and surrendered Shakiah to her.

"But I will always be part of her life," I more asked than stated over the phone. "Promise?"

Rory's grandmother told me what I wanted to hear so she could get Shakiah. And I went to college.

Chapter VI

Food

I found out on accident. I'd overeaten (my go-to breadsticks with ranch and marinara, breadstick after breadstick after breadstick) and I got sick. My stomach started to swell and the nausea kicked in. I rushed to the bathroom and knelt down in front of the toilet and put my finger down my throat to help it all come back out. I vomited hard, vomiting up every single breadstick and all the ranch and marinara I'd just eaten. And, you know what? I felt a whole lot better. And my stomach was a whole lot flatter.

"Hmm," I thought. "What the heck have I just discovered?"

And that was the start of my eating disorder. The start of me being able to eat as much as a I could, and more, and get away with it. Suck it down and puke it right back up like nothing had happened. I got to enjoy my food addiction and not get bigger. It seemed like a miracle. It seemed innocent, almost natural even. I mean, that first time I hadn't even intended on binging and purging. It just happened naturally. So I justified it.

I would eat everything. A whole bunch of everything. The go-to was breadsticks, yeah, but anything I wanted I now knew I could eat it up and spit it back out. I could get the taste, my fix, and then be rid of it. All I had to do was kneel in front of the porcelain goddess and stick my fingers down my throat. I became a full-on bulimic.

From late in high school 'til early in college, this became my addiction. It became my behavior. And the more I did it, the easier it was to do it. It felt like magic. A little bit like cheating, yeah, but also like magic—like I was smarter than the rest. Like I had figured something out, my own little trick. My own little secret.

*

Then, as a sophomore in college, I went for a routine visit to the dentist. To get my teeth cleaned.

"Lindsey," the dentist said after my appointment, "the enamel on your back teeth is wearing thin."

I knew what he was talking about—the acid from the vomit. We talked a bit more, and I admitted what I was doing.

Call it vanity, call it what you want, but I had seen the effect of drug use on people's teeth in my family, and I didn't want to look like them. I didn't want to be flawed when I smiled. I loved my smile. And I couldn't bear to have that Scarlett Letter showing on my teeth. I didn't want to look 'used up.' So I stopped. After that visit to the dentist, I never binged and purged again. Not because I thought it was wrong, but because I didn't want it to affect my appearance.

I got over my addiction. I stopped. I did come to see that it was wrong. That I was harming myself. If I wanted breadsticks with ranch and marinara, now, I'd have to pay the price for it. No more cheating.

Chapter VII

Roadside Assistance

I'm a freshman in college and I have a few friends. I pile five of us into my tiny little Chevy Lumina and drive to Guthrie Center to see Shakiah and go to the county fair. The car is a bundle of young, female energy. We're laughing and joking and having a grand ol' time. Then, headed down the interstate, something's not right with the car. It's sputtering up and down the hills. It's still an hour farther but were determined to get there. The Lumina sputtered on.

"It's getting worse," my friend said from the backseat.

"We're not going to make it."

"Look, a gas station up ahead."

I put on my blinker and took the exit. We pulled up to the Wing's Gas Station in Avoca, Iowa.

"Uh, hello," I said to the guy behind the counter. "My car's breaking down—do you guys have a mechanic?"

"No one on site, but I can get you the number to the travel mechanic. He'll come out here and take a look."

"Okay," I said.

I called the number and in about fifteen minutes, the mechanic pulled up in his truck. He took a quick look at the engine of the Lumina. He looked masculine in the afternoon light. He shut the hood and walked over to me. "You're gonna have to bring it back to the shop," he said, his voice deep and slow. "It's the catalytic converter, we're gonna have to see if we can get a replacement. Could be a few hours."

"Okay," I said. "I just don't know how much I can pay you."

"Let me see what I can do."

The masculine mechanic ended up not being able to get the replacement part—but he cut a hole in the catalytic converter so the air could flow. A temporary fix, for sure, but it allowed us to continue on our girls' weekend.

"Stop by the shop on your way back home," he said, his eyes looking directly into mine.

I could tell he was flirting. I was too; I didn't have any money and I needed my car fixed. "Oh, thank you. Thank you so much."

We made it down to Guthrie Center. I got to introduce Shakiah to my friends, and we had a great time at the Labor Day weekend County Fair.

We packed our bags and hopped back in the Lumina and drove back to the shop on our return drive on Monday, when the mechanic told us the replacement part would be in. I remember being in the office with him, looking at his dirtied hands and the stubble on his face. He charged me $10. Ten dollars! For what must have been a couple hundred-dollar fix.

I gave him ten dollars and my phone number. And, wouldn't you know it, I had a new boyfriend. His name was Shannon.

He was mine. He loved me. He was constantly texting, constantly sending me flowers, constantly surprising me with impromptu visits at my college, constantly taking me on dates, constantly giving me everything that I had ever wanted. He wined and dined me. Maybe a few other things. It was everything that I never knew. It was amazing.

Shannon was a few years older than me. Six, I think. And he had a couple kids from a previous marriage: Terrance, a two-and-a-half-year-old rugrat, and Abigail, a little curly haired ginger tot. It was easy for me to step into the mom roll, and I did. I loved those kids. I loved Shannon. I moved out of the dorms and moved in with him and the children.

*

It was like life finally gave me something. It had taken so much from me. And now it was finally giving me something. A family. A new family.

But, just like before, when things looked good in my young life, that's when the bottom was about to drop.

Abby started exhibiting some red-flag behaviors. Then Terrance came to visit from his mom's place in Iowa, and he was covered in bruises from his head to toe. I asked him some questions. And, yep, what I thought was happening *was* happening. They were being abused. I knew I couldn't sit back and let him continue to get beaten, so I made the call to Child Protective Services. It was a long, drawn-out battle across state lines and through red tape, but, in the end, Shannon and I were awarded full custody of Terrance and Abby. They came to live with us full time. As a family, we went through a lot of recovery and healing. So much trauma all around.

During it all, Shannon and I had gotten married and conceived our own son, Jayden. We'd bought a home. Our home. White picket fence and all. We had dogs. Even a swimming pool. I was a senior in college, a wife, a full-time mother of three—it was like I had recreated my life as a senior in high school.

"Maybe this is my destiny," I thought. But life had more in store for me.

Chapter VIII

Here We Go Again

Terrance had become a rambunctious little five-year-old, running around the house and just full of 'little boy energy.' Abby was a handful too. I don't remember exactly what happened, but one day Terrance and Abby had gotten into trouble. Probably for fighting or just not listening to mom. I got them into the living room to have to give them a little talking to.

My dad's way of punishing me and my siblings and half-siblings when we were young was, if we'd gotten into a tiff or something, he'd make us put on one of his XXL T-shirts—both of us, we'd have to get inside of it, stay inside of it, and he'd put us in the recliner chair and make us just sit there together. It was an awful punishment really. And, now as a mom, I was like, well "maybe this is what I'm supposed to do?" Some sort of weird conditioning or something.

So Terrance and Abby got into trouble and I thought that this was what I should do. I put them in an adult T-shirt and said, "You will sit there together and think about what you just did. I'm going to give Jayden his bath and then I'll come back and talk about what you've learned.

So I went and gave Jayden his bath and then dried him and tucked him into bed, thinking all the while what a great mother I am. Well, I got back into the living room to give Terrance and Abby their talkin' to and I turn the corner and see them: and they are in a position that no four-year-old and eighteen-month-old should even know about, let alone be in—an 'adult' position.

Right then, it hit me: I knew they'd been more than just physically abused. They'd experienced much more; their abuse had gotten sexual.

I had two choices. I could break down and go back into a shell of human that I'd reverted to at times in my life or I could put my foot down and be strong for them. For myself and for them. I could teach them that what they'd experienced at the hand of their mother (I found out it had been her) was not right. That they didn't have to be victims of their circumstance. Not anymore.

*

Meanwhile, Shannon had taken a job that took him away from the home during the week, and I was alone with three young babies figuring out how to be a mom. How to mother. It wasn't easy.

Then, well then, I started to notice Shannon getting out of bed real early in the morning. Like super early, and he was being all sneaky about it. I also started getting these notices that the credit cards were maxed out. I didn't know where the money was being spent; it sure wasn't me. These two coincidences proved to be anything but.

Things around the house got tense.

"What are you spending the money on?" I asked him.

He never gave much of a response. I didn't figure out where all of it was going, but I did some digging and found out where some of it was going. He'd been getting out of bed super early for a reason. To go to porn sites. Expensive ones.

He wasn't waking up early to be intimate with his wife. He was sneaking out of bed in the wee hours to watch pornography. He was becoming some sort of sex addict.

And then it got worse.

In November of that year, 2006, I went in for my annual woman's appointment at the doctor. I thought nothing of it. Routine stuff, and I headed out to go to a retreat to receive an award for Coordinator of the Year at my job working with troubled kids at something called The Diversion Program. I was I'm about to get called on stage I see a missed call on my phone. It was the doctor's office. I checked the voicemail.

"Hello, Lindsey, this is Dr. Sarah's office. We've received some test results back and we'd like to see you back in the office. Give us a call as soon as you can."

My heart did a double beat. What was this about? I called them back.

Chlamydia. They told me that I had contracted chlamydia. I'd been married for over three years and had been 100% faithful to my husband—and all of a sudden I have chlamydia?

"Doc," I said, "I mean, could it have come from the toilet seat or something?"

I was really that naïve. It didn't occur to me that my husband could have gotten it and given it to me. I was *that* blind.

I hung up the phone and went back into the conference and gathered my wits. I went on stage, got my award and I left. I went straight home. My husband was still out of town on work. I called him.

"I know what you did," I said. "I know what you've been up to."

I heard a gulp on the other end of the phone, but Shannon went and flat-out denied it. I knew right then I would leave him. It was incredibly difficult because I knew that meant not seeing Terrance and Abby on a daily basis. But I knew I simply could not stay with this man. I could not stay with Shannon.

I made Shannon promise that, despite us divorcing, I would always be in Terrance and Abby's life. He did. He made that promise. And I moved out. I was rid of that man.

*

The divorce got messy. I left him but the divorce would not come through quickly. He'd maxed out all the credit cards and there was massive debt because of it. We had every card you could think of: Walmart, Sears, Chase, Mastercard, Visa, you name it.

I got a call from my lawyer one day saying, "Lindsey, we have bad news. Shannon has filed for bankruptcy."

To not get stuck with all the marital debt—it was close to a million dollars—my lawyer told me I'd have to file for bankruptcy. Shannon had been using a high percentage of his income from that new job to wine and dine his mistresses out on the road. Late nights at the bar, hotel rooms, sex sites on the internet, that's where the money was going—and if I wasn't careful, I was going to get stuck with all the debt from it.

Life, it wasn't easy back then.

I hung up with my lawyer and it hit me like an earthquake. I was devastated. I had worked so hard. So hard to get the white picket fence and have all the things for my children, to get my degree, to get out of the shit from my childhood and get my life going—and then it was gone in a flash.

We had to jointly file for bankruptcy. I lost my car. I lost my home. I was back at square one, back at the starting point. I'd have to do it all over again.

Chapter IX

The Terrible Saga of the Man Named Charlie

Part One

I decided to go back home to Guthrie Center for my friend Chelsie's college graduation party. I wanted to have some fun: translation, I wanted to find the cutest boy at the party and then have some fun. I found him, and we did. We had a great night together. A one-night stand with all the fixins. His name was Charlie, and he was charismatic and fun. We had our night together, and in the morning, I said goodbye to him and thanked him for a lovely evening. I never thought I'd see him again.

I left Guthrie Center and drove back to my crumbled life in Nebraska to work out the details of my divorce and get my life back on track financially and emotionally.

Two weeks went by and I started to think about the guy from that night, and I sent him a funny text.

"Oh my gosh," he replied. "I didn't think I was ever going to hear from you again. I've been thinking so much about you. I would really like to see you again sometime."

His response gave me a smile. It did. But I thought, there's no way I need to jump right back into a relationship—my divorce isn't even finalized!

But then, reality set in. My reality. I didn't have home. I didn't have enough money to live on. The alimony hadn't even kicked in yet and with the divorce dragging on it wouldn't be for some time. I didn't know how I was going to support Jayden.

I fell into it—into my mom's story, into codependency. Into going from one man to the next for support. I did, I admit it. Charlie owned his own barber shop and was making good money and he told me he would take care of me and Jayden. He promised he would, and I fell for it—hook, line and sinker.

*

Charlie had a way about him, and he drew me in. We had fun together. The romance was good. The intensity was there. But, not too far into that dating-honeymoon I discovered he had a problem with alcohol. A pretty severe one. He exhibited signs of alcoholism, and I was frightened; I had seen too much of it from my mother and father to enter into a relationship with someone showing such symptoms of the disease.

He needed to get help; and, before I was going to move back to Guthrie Center and be with him full-go I asked him to get it. I gave him the ultimatum: "If we're going to do this, you need to seek out some treatment. You need to go to rehab."

And you know what? He did. What a feeling it was for me, like, wow, this man really does love me. He's willing to get help. He's willing to do what I need him to do, willing to become the man I need him to become.

He agreed to enter a treatment facility for 28 days. And when he came out of it, things *were* different. Things were amazing. I thought Charlie was going to be 'the one.' I really did.

A few weeks later, I went to the doctor to refill my birth control.

"Lindsey," the doctor said, "I have to ask. Is there any way you could be pregnant?"

"What? No, doc. I've been taking my pill."

"Okay, but before I refill your prescription, we're going to do a pregnancy test just to be sure. I heard what you said, but it's standard procedure—dangerous on the off chance there is a developing fetus."

We did the test and the doctor went to another room to obtain the results. I waited in the room and scrolled through my phone. The door opened and the doctor walked back in.

"Lindsey," he said through what looked like a forced smile, "congratulations are in order. You're pregnant."

"No fucking way I am."

He just looked at me and nodded his head slowly. "Yes, I believe you are."

Shit shit shit shit shit. I wasn't even officially divorced. I'm 24 years old and can barely afford to take care of Jayden. Charlie and I hadn't been sexual too often, I mean he'd been away at rehab for most of our young time together. I guess there was that one time we snuck around the treatment center.

Life.

The initial shock wore off, and very quickly I became very excited. Another child! A new family with a new man. I had the doctor put the pregnancy test inside one of those biohazard bags and went to Ben Franklin and got a little card that said, "Congratulations Daddy!" I was so excited. I drove to Charlie's barber shop, right as he was closing up. I wanted to surprise him and give him the news and his card. I thought he would be ecstatic.

He wasn't. And it was obvious. And that started his spiral out of sobriety and back into the deep abyss of alcoholism.

Charlie went back to the bottle and our relationship became nothing but argument after argument, fight after fight. I'm talking loud words and violent, physical altercations.

I was pregnant with Jhetta. She would be born a few months after that visit to the doctor. At that time, Charlie got bad. He had forgotten all about his promise of sobriety to me. He started going out at night. Soon, it was every night. I'm at home, pregnant, and my man is out partying. It sucked.

One night he even passed out in the neighbor's yard. Our neighbor found him there the next day. Late in the morning, already like 94 degrees out, and he put a fan on him and just let him sleep it off.

"Just Charlie being Charlie," he told me after the fact.

Yeah, well I wanted Charlie to be the Charlie I *needed* him to be. The Charlie who Jayden and our new daughter needed him to be.

It wasn't meant to be.

Rumors started around town that he was cheating on me. Tiny, little midwestern town rumors that, at first, I didn't believe. Maybe my mind just blocked me from believing. I'm not sure. But it soon became apparent he was, with his old baby mama. Yep.

The Terrible Saga of the Man Named Charlie

Part Two

The first time he put his hands on me and got physical and I remember running the staircases in our house. They were these unique staircases where you could go up one side and down the other, sort of run a circle through the house. I used them. I had to. I remember running up one side and down the other, running out of fear, running to stay away from him.

"I can't end up like my mom," I told myself one day after he'd hit me. "I can't stick around through this shit. I'm out."

I knew I couldn't fix the situation. I couldn't fix Charlie and I couldn't fix 'me and Charlie.' But what I could fix was myself.

I had interned at the Women's Crisis Center back in college. And in one of those terrified moments running away from Charlie, it was this patient of mine's words that I kept hearing. She'd asked me to "fix the inside" of her. This person had bruises all over her face and body, but told me, "those will go away. What I need you to do is help me fix what's inside."

The words rang true. I couldn't fix the external circumstances. But I could fix whatever it was inside of me that kept attracting me to unhealthy relationships. I had to.

So I set out on this journey. I knew I could do it. I'd got a great job as Chief Deputy Assessor for Guthrie County. I was young. I had enough motivation and enough money. I didn't need a man. I came to see that I could do it on my own.

It was 2008 and I moved out of Charlie's house. Got my own place. But, because of my job, I had to still be in the same town as him. I'd see him around every once in a while, like at the grocery store and such. Sometimes I'd get a call from the bartender that "Charlie was in one of his stupors" and that someone needed to drive him home. He had no one else, and so I would. I was too nice. Too forgiving. I should have shunned Charlie completely.

Then, one night, one rainy Iowa night, I'm sitting next to my window being a mom to my children and texting with a friend. I never closed the blinds by that couch because literally no one could see inside unless they walked around my side yard and looked in from there. I was laying on the couch and I got an eerie feeling that someone was watching me. That disgusting feeling that I was being watched. I couldn't shake it. I walked over to the blinds and shut them. First time I'd ever shut them.

I walked outside to sneak a cigarette. I'd cut down drastically with the pregnancy, but just couldn't stop completely and I'd get a few drags in the evening. I went out to the patio table. There were way more cigarettes in the ashtray than what I'd smoked. I reached onto the table and picked up my pack; it was a fresh pack and half were gone. Right then I got a text message: "I see you."

It was from Charlie.

I looked around, wide eyed. I couldn't see anyone. My heart beat fast.

"Charlie! What the hell are you doing?! Come out!"

From out the shadows, like a werewolf, he appeared. He walked closer and I took a step back.

"I just want to talk with you," he said. "I just want to have a conversation."

I could tell he was sober. That, somehow, made me feel safe. "Sure. Yes, yes, come sit down. Let's talk."

He told me how sorry he was and how he wanted to be part of Jhetta's life when she was born. I fell for it. I wanted to believe him and so I did. Over the course of the summer, I let Charlie back into my life. We never moved back in together, but we started hanging out a bit.

One night in August he stayed overnight. We got out of bed and both of us got ready for work. We were walking out the front door into what seemed like just another day—and I felt the contractions.

I went back inside the house to gather myself. I took a few deep breaths. I came back out to the patio: "Charlie, I think my water just broke!"

The hospital was 45 minutes away. Charlie gets in the driver's seat, speeds over to the barber shop and puts a "Baby on Way—Shop Closed" sign on the door and we were on the highway bound for the natal unit.

We arrived at the hospital. "I'm having a bab-ay!" I screamed to the first person who'd listen. "Right. Dang. Now!"

They got me onto a gurney and into a room. I was having excruciating pain. I felt this instant gush of fluid, a puddle of ooze. I called the nurse in and said, "I think my water just broke more."

The nurse came in and patted my face down and cleaned me up. She pulled the covers up over me. I was looking at her as she did it. I was looking at her as the color drained from her face.

"Lindsey," she said quickly, "One moment—" And she picked up the phone, dialing some sort of code into it. A doctor showed up almost immediately, as if she'd run over. She completely removed the sheets from around my body— and I saw it, the bed, covered in blood.

My first thought, well it wasn't so much of a thought as the worst imaginable fear of a mother: my baby rejected me.

"We may be in a dire situation here, Lindsey," the doctor said. "It could just be a blood vessel, but we don't know yet. We're going to watch you very closely, but in the meantime, we need to prep you in case we need to go into emergency C-Section."

My baby was still alive.

But blood was oozing out, more of it every second. On the bed, pooling on the floor, everywhere.

Moments passed like days. The doctor came back in. "Your placenta is abrupt—we're taking you in for an emergency C-Section."

"Right now?"

"We have three minutes to save your life and the life of your child."

The team yanked me out of the room and rushed me down the hall to Emergency. The anesthesiologist was literally straddling the table as it was being pushed down the hallway trying to get the mask on me and put me under. My last memory was my arms tied down and the mask going on. I ripped it from my face.

"Lindsey, we're going to lose you! Let me do my job!"

I let him. The last thing I remember was saying, "I don't care if I die—just save my baby."

Moments later, Jhetta was born. But I was not awake to meet her, to be there with her, to bond with her. I woke from surgery twelve hours later and met her for the first time. It was a weird feeling, knowing she had already been in this world for a half-day without me. She'd already been named. Other people had touched her, other people had bonded with her. But not me.

The first time I held her, I remember feeling no connection. Those twelve hours had created some sort of chasm between us, and I started postpartum depression. From the onset, I did not want to be around my child. It would resolve itself, and I am so in love with her now, but initially it was a very difficult thing for a mother to go through.

*

Months passed. Life was lived and Thanksgiving came around, and Charlie and I were supposed to go back home to Nebraska and introduce her and Jayden to them. We had it all planned out and we were literally about to start the drive when he got a call from the mother of his other child.

She told him something like, "Your daughter wants to see you. If you want to see her, you need to come out to my house."

"I mean," I said to him, "you're coming with us, right?"

No, he wasn't. He chose his other family over ours. I told him never to come back to our house. I felt like I had just been stabbed in the back.

Later that day, he called me. "Where are you?" I asked.

"I'm home," he said.

"Home? What home? I told you never to go back there!"

"Lindsey!" he snarled, and I could tell he'd been drinking, "if you don't come back home right now, I'm kicking in this fucking door!"

I knew he was capable of it. I also knew I wasn't going. I hung up the phone and called the police officer in town. "Matt, can you do me a favor. Go check my house. Charlie's threatening to kick down the door and destroy my home. I'm two hours away. Can you please just go check it out?"

"Yeah, Lindsey, no problem. I'm sure everything's fine, but I'll check on it for you."

Twenty-minutes later, Matt called back: "Lindsey, we're going to need you to come back home. Charlie is in your home; he's kicked in the door. There's destruction everywhere. We're gonna need you to come back home."

So I loaded up my newborn and my toddler and I drove at midnight on Thanksgiving, to find my home kicked up, ransacked, destroyed.

The Terrible Saga of the Man named Charlie

Part Three

January comes around, and I'm feeling like I'm succumbing to postpartum depression again. I'm really struggling to keep up at work and I'm struggling to do much other than take care of my children. I wanted to do it all on my own, but I was struggling. I needed someone. I didn't have anyone to call, no one except Charlie. So I did it. I called him. I can't believe I did, but I called him.

"I need your help," I said. "I need you to be sober and I need you to come help with the kids. Please."

He put on his Dr. Jekyll face and came over and was the good person he could be from time to time. I began to trust him again. I know now how stupid I was. It was obviously a huge mistake.

One weekend we'd promised Jayden we'd take him sledding, at Sunny Hollow outside of Des Moines. We got Jhetta over to her grandma's; and Charlie, his other daughter, Jayden, and I set out for a fun day, a good day. It turned into about the worst day imaginable. First, we get to the sled hill and they tell us that the kids are too young, that "five-year-old's are too young. They can't go."

I tried to talk the lady out of it, but she wouldn't budge. I told the kids how sorry I was, and that we would take them sledding on a hill back home. We piled back into the car and started the return drive.

Jayden wasn't having it. We'd promised him sledding at Sunny Hollow and he wanted his sledding at

Sunny Hollow. He didn't understand why he couldn't go, and he lost his shit.

"Let me out of the car!" he kept saying. "I want to go sledding now!"

Charlie snapped. He turned around in his seat and I saw a blackness in his eyes. His death-stare. He grabbed Jayden by the coat and started shaking him violently. His death-stare was deep, his eyes black and distant and cruel.

He smashed Jayden's head into the back window of the pickup and then it whiplashed forward and struck the seat, hard.

I went into a mother's rage to protect my child. "Stop, Charlie! Stop!!"

Charlie craned his neck and turned towards me. The death-stare, those black, murderous eyes penetrating mine. He smashed my face into the side window. Dazed, I picked up my phone and got off a quick text to a friend. I dialed 9-1-1 and it rang once before Charlie grabbed the phone from me and hung it up.

We're on the backroads and there is ice on them, and Charlie is driving like a maniac. Both children in the back seat are screaming, begging for mercy. I thought we might die in a fiery crash.

*

Maybe the text I got off and the disconnected 9-1-1 call had the police looking for us? I hoped so. But I didn't know. I didn't know where we were or what was going to happen. We were in the hands of a madman, a crazed man with a death-stare in his eye. My kids were frantic, and I was so scared.

"Jayden," Charlie says, possessed. "Do you want to watch your mom die today?"

He told my son he was going to kill me in an abandoned church, and that no one would miss me.

I pleaded with him, I begged him. "I won't tell the cops. Charlie, I won't tell anyone. No one ever has to know about this. Just let us out of the car."

I prayed to God. I asked angels to protect us. I vowed, no matter, what, to leave this man once and for all.

"Let us out of the car," I said, and there was something in my voice, a firmness and resolve from the core of my being.

Somehow, we didn't die. The car didn't crash into flames. My throat wasn't slit in an abandoned church. Jayden didn't get his skull bashed in. The death-stare lightened, just a touch, and the madman let us out of the car. On the side of the road, wherever we were, we were finally safe.

*

Charlie was charged with serious domestic assault causing injury. He was charged with the felony. And I got away from that madman.

But there was one more crucible to pass. One more episode with Charlie. I'd gone out for drinks with some girlfriends a few weeks later. Just to feel normal. And that madman showed up at the bar. I saw him out of a corner eye and paid my tab and left quickly. I couldn't bear to be in the same room as him.

I went home and crawled into bed and tried to forget it. Then, just as I was drifting off to sleep, I felt something, someone, crawl into bed behind me. It was Charlie.

"Leave my home!" I screamed. "Get out of my house!"

He was drunk and he wanted sex. That is all that he wanted. He wanted sex and his mad mind was made up that he was going to get sex.

I fought back. He started punching me in the back of the head. He began kicking me in the kidneys and in my back. He smashed my hand on the marble nightstand. It was a nightmare.

I darted out of the bed and managed to get a few feet of separation from him. I ran downstairs. I grabbed the keys to the van, ran outside and locked myself inside. I picked up my phone and called a friend.

"Charlie is here!" I said through heavy breaths. "Get someone over here. Now!"

Friends ran over from the bar. It wasn't too far away, and they showed up quickly. The cops showed up—but Jesse, Charlie's best friend, is the cop that arrived. And he didn't arrest him!

"Let's get you out of here!" he said to Charlie, and they left. He protected the man who had just broken into my house and beat the hell out of me.

Two other deputies show up at my house. They sat with me that night and took my story. They assured me they would protect me, that they'd watch my house, that they'd keep us safe. But I knew Charlie wasn't in jail. I knew he was out there somewhere. And I knew what he was capable of.

I went into a state of what later would be a diagnosis of PTSD. Six days without sleeping. Constant alert. Constant nervousness. Constant terror. I didn't get into bed without a machete under my pillow.

I was broken. It was time I started fixing myself. Fixing the inside of myself so the outside circumstances wouldn't ever be like this again. It was time I started to break the cycle that had been handed to me by my parents.

The past was a dark cloud. I needed to see some blue skies in my future. I had to. My children needed me to. *I* needed me to.

"My children needed me. I needed me, too."

Chapter X

Good Men, Finally

Time passed. Life moved on. I was getting stronger. Friends were helping me, and they told me that I needed to have some fun. To start enjoying life again. I told them I would. And when I went to my stepbrother's wedding at 1316 Jones Street in Omaha, I decided to do so. I went there with a positive frame of mind. I didn't go there to meet a man. I just went there to celebrate. And, as fate would prove, that was enough to meet a good man.

In the late afternoon sun, I saw the most beautiful man walking into the wedding reception.

"Who is that?" I asked a relative.

"Lindsey, that is Ryan. He's a good man, and he's married. Don't corrupt him—leave him alone."

As much improvement as I'd made in my outlook and the way I was living life, I was still no saint. Later that night with a little help from some liquid courage, I walked right up to him—his hazel-green eyes and his electric smile, and my mouth started to speak for me: "I'm marrying you," I told him. "Today."

"That may be difficult. See, I'm married."

And, although he maintained loyalty to his marriage vows (I later learned they were in a huge fight and, indeed, were on the outs) we had a super fun night together. He treated me with respect, and he made me laugh. The entire evening, we were never too far away from each other. But at the end of the reception, we went our separate ways. But it felt like some sort of seed was planted, like maybe down the line, if the stars   aligned.

*

In the meantime, the stars led me to another good man—one who *wasn't* married. His name was Mitch, and he fell in love with me and took my children in like they were his own. For three years, he was the only Daddy that Jhetta ever knew.

Mitch and I grounded our relationship, first and foremost, as friends. We were the best of friends. He was such a good man. But that spark, that intense romance, never really quite formed.

Mitch was a farm boy. And he wanted to remain a farm boy. I wanted 'more,' for better or worse, and I knew our time, though good, would be limited.

I remember sitting in church one Sunday morning in 2012 or so—first time I'd set foot in a church in years—and the pastor's sermon was all about marriage and God's plan, like "if you're in a relationship, one year to two years in and marriage is not on the horizon then marriage isn't happening, and so that person is not in God's plan for you."

I started to cry. It was like the pastor was talking straight at me. Because, though to this day Mitch is still one of my best friends, we were never soulmates. That Sunday afternoon, I got home from Church and started doing the dishes, my mind heavy. I was standing at the sink and Mitch came up behind me and put his arms around me and gave me a big hug.

When I felt his touch, I knew I couldn't do it anymore. I couldn't do this to Mitch anymore. I told him how I felt. I told him that I loved him but that I didn't feel we were meant to be together forever. He was hurt. (So was

I.) But after a long conversation he came to see what I saw. Mitch and I had a good time together, but it was over.

God had a different plan for me.

That night, that very night, I was sitting on the couch and scrolling though Facebook to take my mind off the day. There was a message. It was from Ryan! "Lindsey," it read, "we met one night three years ago, and I've done nothing but think about you since." The same day I knew Mitch and I weren't meant to be together forever I got this message from the universe. I'd trusted my instincts and, it seemed, the universe had been listening.

Mitch went on to find his soulmate and have three beautiful children of his own. And me? Ryan and I got hot and steamy together pretty darn quick. It must have been in the stars.

Within three months of that Facebook message, Ryan and I had moved in together in Omaha. We started a life together. And, this time, this man, it felt right.

It felt so right that we didn't feel the need to jump right into marriage. We waited for about four years, just enjoying each other and allowing Jayden and Jhetta get comfortable with having a new Daddy. After years of good times and a growing love, we finally set a date: May 14, 2016.

The night Ryan and I met in 2009

*

That moment, the wedding, I felt was the time to make amends with my parents; I wanted my dad to walk me down the aisle. And I wanted my mom to be at my wedding.

Looking back, I'm not sure if it was such a great idea. That decision brought a lot of toxic things back into my life. I started to suffer anxiety again. I hadn't in so long, but just thinking about my parents and my past brought it right back. Ryan had been so good; life had been so good. And now, with the memories and toxicity of my parents coming back into my life, I started to feel the nervousness again. I was diagnosed with a panic disorder, and I ended up being hospitalized for a couple days. I got out and it happened again. It seemed like I was going to the hospital with panic attacks every other day. I just couldn't get the weight off my chest, couldn't get the elephant off my body. There were times when I couldn't breathe, and I felt certain I was dying.

To top it all off, my brother—the man who sexually assaulted me throughout my childhood—had been released from prison. Just knowing he was out, that he could get to me if he wanted to, put me over the edge.

It shames me to admit this, but I started eating Xanax by the handful. Just trying to feel normal, trying to feel human, trying to feel like 'myself.' I see now how stupid it was, but at the time it felt like my only option; I couldn't keep going in and out of the hospital. It was too hard on Ryan and the kids.

My grandmother wanted my brother to be at the wedding.

"100% no way," I told her.

"You are an awful human being," she said.

Yep.

So we had the wedding and because I forbid my brother from being there, a lot of my other family refused to show up. So be it—other people in my life did. Other amazing people I'd met throughout my life drove from all over the place to be at my wedding. And, walking down the aisle that afternoon, I was sure that Ryan was the one. I was sure that God had brought us together. He was the support I needed. I didn't need the toxicity of my old family. I needed the pillar that was Ryan and the strength of moving forward with my new family. I was sure I was living God's plan. I was. Finally.

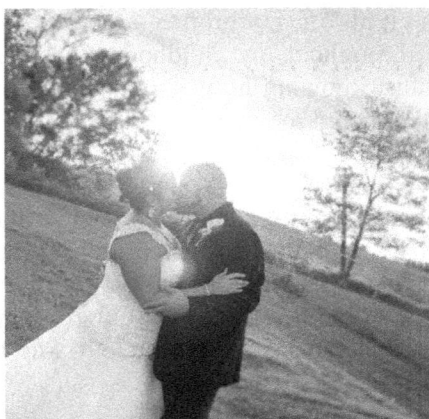
My Wedding Day with Ryan

Chapter XI

Innocence

It's first grade and me and my sister, Carrie are best friends. Our teacher is trying to teach us things but we can't pay attention. In story time, we can't even hear her words. Because we're already in our swimsuits with our towels draped around our shoulders and as soon as that whistle blows, we're heading to the city pool.

The bell rang, and we were out of that classroom and into the spring sunshine of Gretna, Nebraska faster than a tornado. We hopped on our bikes and rode under a deep blue sky with smiles plastered on our faces. Just giggling and being silly girls, happy.

We made it to the pool and parked our bikes and made it through the gate and jumped into the water. It felt good against my skin. Carrie was a ball of laughter.

We played mermaids—and we felt like we were in Never Never Land. Our troubles were a million miles away.

We melted our Now-and-Laters in the sun, stretching the cow tails into a gooey mess of goodness. We slurped down our cherry-dipped ice cones in a hurry so they wouldn't melt.

We got out our pennies and rubbed them in the concrete to turn them silver and pass them off as dimes.

"You think they'll catch us?" Carrie asked.

"Naahhhh," I said, and we both grinned the grin of the first grader, missing teeth and innocence.

The sun was warm and the water cool. It was me and my sister. It was a good day. One we never wanted to end.

Chapter XII

Death and Resurrection

Fast forward about a decade to 2014. Another pivotal year in the destiny of my life. My grandfather died. Then my uncle died because he couldn't take the loss of his father. My uncle killed himself. He lost the will to live. Because of this:

My phone rang at two o'clock in the morning. Never good. It was my aunt. They said they had been looking for my uncle. That he'd gone missing. They'd been calling him but it was going straight to voicemail. They sleuthed his Facebook for clues. Nothing. She asked me if I knew anything, if I'd "heard from him?"

"No," I answered. "I haven't."

"Well, let us know if you hear anything. And I'll call you back if we find anything out."

I should have turned off my phone. Because it rang again. Not even an hour later.

"They found him," my aunt said, and her voice was grim. "You need to come over right away."

I drove to the parking lot where his truck had been found. My uncle was inside it, dead. He'd put on layers of clothing; layers of hats so there wouldn't be a mess. The gun, I saw, still lay on his chest.

The medical personnel hadn't even arrived yet. It was just policemen trying to coral the scene. I remember being incredibly cold, shivering, when I looked into the cab and saw my uncle, his dead body, the blood. But I couldn't pull myself away. I just kept looking at him. Eventually an officer came over and stepped between me and the sight of my uncle. We waited for the coroner to come. I kept moving side-to-side to see him, to continue to look at him. I don't know why, but I couldn't look away from the horror film.

The coroner finally showed up and this tiny little female cop stepped in front of me, blocking my sight.

"You need to move," I growled. "It's my uncle—move!"

"Honey," she said with a tenderness in her voice, "you don't want to see this."

"I need to—"

But she cut me off, and I stepped back. I was only 20 feet or so from my uncle, from his body, when they struggled to get him out of the truck and into the body bag. I heard the thud of his body hitting the pavement. The sound of the zipper as they zipped him up. And for the next nine months, every time the refrigerator door closed, or I zipped my kid's coats up for school I was brought back to that parking lot at four in the morning. The horror film reel. The cold, shivering panic. The not being able to look away. The death.

My uncle's life had gotten so bad that he made the decision to end it. I hoped he found what he was looking for. And that's when the thoughts of suicide, of a way out, reentered my mind in a big way. But not yet.

I had to keep living. My life was not perfect, my life had been hard; I had been beaten and battered from people and from fate, but I had to keep living. I couldn't be like my uncle. Though I was tempted, I wouldn't be like my uncle.

I buried the pain deep so no one would know. My aunt and my stepmom needed me. I had to be their strength, so I couldn't show weakness. I was the one they leaned on, in that moment of loss, to give them a sort of grounding. A sort of sturdy footing.

That was me. 'Sturdy footing.' Someone to be strong, to not show my emotions, someone to be walked on, if necessary, to keep the family together. That was me.

And I got good at it. From all that practice as a little girl through all that shit in high school and college, and now my uncle had killed himself. Death all around.

Things went from bad to worse.

My Cousin, Lucas, from the other side of the family, was going in for his one weekend a month in the National Guard. But he didn't show up.

I'd grown up with Lucas. We had scraped our knees together, eaten ice cream together. And he hadn't shown up for the Guard. We all got phone calls. The mood was eerie and silent.
Had he wrecked his car? Had he gone AWOL?

"Have you heard from him?"

"Have you seen him?"

No one had.

A search party went out. We were all asked the last time we saw him and what his behavior pattern had been. He'd been sick for a time, depressed and overall, not very good. That much came out.

He never did show up for his weekend at the National Guard. He became a 'Missing Person.' We were worried. All of us. We expected the worst. I know I did. And then, our greatest fears were realized. A few days later he was found at the family farm. Dead. He had taken his own life. He had killed himself. My cousin had committed suicide right after my uncle had committed suicide. The tears flowed.

I remember the service. The Marine Corps came out and the funeral was actually quite beautiful. A beautiful end to a tragic life. We were all standing outside the church. I can still see the Marines saluting Luca's cremation box. It felt so strange, so strange but I had this feeling like I needed to take a photograph. I needed a picture of this moment. So I took out my phone and snapped a photo of the Marines saluting my cousin. Little Lucas who'd grown up to be a man and who now was dead.

I felt this impulse, deep inside or from elsewhere, to take a picture of the moment. I did.

The ceremony ended and we all went our separate ways. I took out my phone and looked at the photograph I'd taken, and this is what I saw: angel wings, clearly outlined, all around me in brilliant white.

I couldn't believe it. Until I could. I felt calm, calm and empowered. It was permission, some sort of 'permission from beyond,' the universe telling me that I am surrounded by the arms of angels, that I could do what I needed to do, that I could be there for my family and lift them up, that I knew Lucas was in a good place and that I had the celestial support to take care of my family here on earth.

I had always believed in angels. Through all the shit I'd been through, through all the shit my family had been through, through all the shit that Lucas had been through, I'd always believed. And here they were. Angels, all around me.

Little did I know how much I would need their help.

Chapter XIII

Hell

A year and a half later. Mother's Day 2017. Shakiah called and she said, "Hi Mom, how are you how are things?"

"Oh, I'm good honey. I miss you. How are you?"

"I miss you too," she said. "I called to say Happy Mother's Day. I love you, mom."

We had a beautiful conversation. She was my daughter. It felt good to talk to her. Then, like the girl she was, she said, "We'll talk to you later," and she hung up the phone.

I fell asleep thinking about life. About my daughter and about my life. I did not sleep well, and in the morning, I started scrolling Facebook, that scroll, and in the scroll I saw a photograph of blackness and flames. Destruction. But I recognized the blackness and flames. What it once was: Shakiah's grandmother's house, Shirley's house, burnt to the ground, in a heap of memory and ash.

I immediately texted my friend Courtney, and she told me that Shirley had got out. That Bill had been life-flighted.

Lindsey, the words came, they haven't found the girls. Neither Shakiah or her cousin Paige. Nothing.

Were they buried in the rubble? Were they safe at a friend's house? I was panic-stricken, my pulse leaping into my sternum. I put down the phone and drove to the Omaha hospital to see Bill and get some answers. Grandma Shirley was there. "What are *you* doing here?"

We'd hadn't seen eye to eye on a lot of things, but now wasn't the time. "Where are the girls?" I said. "Where's Shakiah?"

She just grabbed me. The recent trauma had melted old ice. "Be still," she said calmly. "I need to tell you something."

My heart sank to the deepest pit of the deepest chasm in the deep abyss of human pain. I knew. I knew she had been inside the house when it burnt down. I knew she was gone. I knew Shakiah was gone.

The days trickled by as slow as a pond turns from ice back into its liquid form. Shakiah was dead. I did not know what to do.

We waited to see if Bill would survive. He was in the ICU being treated for symptoms stemming from smoke inhalation. I had taken Shirley to the ER for a broken foot when a DCI investigator walked in, all formal like. I looked at him, trying to understand.

See, Shakiah's cousin Paige, whom she'd been living with in Shirley's home, had been being sexually assaulted by her dad and brother. That's how she ended up living there. Child Protective Services had taken her away from her father and sent her to live with her grandmother. And that Monday, Paige was set to testify personally for permanent placement with her grandmother.

Her older brother made the decision to silence her.

He barricaded the house and then set fire to it. That was his plan. Shakiah had been murdered.

It was too much to bear. For the first time since my childhood, I didn't see a way out. I went home and didn't leave my house. I rarely left my bed. All my relationships started to disintegrate. Especially my relationship to myself. My daughter was gone. My daughter had been murdered. She was innocent. So innocent. What was God's plan? I did not understand. Life was not worth living.

I'd made my decision. On March 26, 2018, I was done. I was going to end it. End my life. It was the only way to stop the pain.

I was driving down the interstate and my mind was made up. I'd made my own plan; I would drive under a semi-truck. I would get crushed, to death, and I would feel no more pain. I would escape this awful thing called life.

I was about to do it. To follow through on a lifetime of suicidal thoughts and finally do it. Then I looked in the rearview mirror. I saw a minivan. A minivan with a family inside. And that stopped me. In a flash I saw the selfishness of what I was going to do—I couldn't take my life and leave my family behind. It all happened so fast. One moment I was certain, absolutely certain I was going to end my life—and then I wasn't. There was more I had to do on this earth.

*

I remember that exit on the interstate to this day. Clear as day. But I don't remember the rest of the drive home. It was as if the angels had come down and guided me back to my driveway. I don't remember any of it. I just remember getting home and walking through the front door and hugging my husband and my children.

"Are you okay, mommy?" they asked.

I wasn't. I went to my bedroom. I tried to sleep but I couldn't shake the nightmares.

"Lord," I said. "Why? Why me? Why my daughter? Why?"

There was no answer.

My nightmares and visions and depression and extreme anxiety worsened. I buried myself in food. I ate myself to over 300 pounds. Days went by in a blur of chaos and food and depression and hating God.

I didn't see a way out. I saw no pathway forward. Until I was offered to try a trial product of something called Happy Coffee...

Chapter XIV

Rebirth

I couldn't shake the nightmares. I couldn't calm myself down. The anxiety and depression were real. I couldn't stop eating. I couldn't stop seeing visions of my Shakiah. I was in the abyss. And *coffee* was going to snap me out of it?

*

The very next day, March 27, 2018, I got in my car again and drove the two hours all the way back down to Guthrie Center to meet with an individual to pick up seven days of this happy coffee she claimed would make me feel better.

"If you honestly try it for seven days and don't feel like it's working for you," she told me, "feel free to go all over Facebook and blast how 'shitty this product is.'"

I already hated this woman. I hated everything at this point in my life. Life. God. Myself. I was hurt to the point of broken. But coffee was better than meth.

She gave me the happy coffee and we said our goodbyes and I drove to the nearest gas station. I put some gasoline in my car and made some coffee for myself. Happy coffee or not, I needed to drive another two hours—and it *was* coffee.

It tasted good and my vehicle and myself were ready for the drive back. I thought a lot as I drove along the interstate, the Iowa cornfields becoming Nebraska cornfields as the sun set in the west and fiery colors played the coming twilight. I made it home and went to sleep.

I slept through the night. The next morning, I made a second glass of the supposedly special coffee. I almost had to stop and think, "wait, I'm out of bed?" It was kind of odd for me to be up and about, moving, being a human. Maybe there *was* something to this coffee?

I had a decently productive day, went to bed, slept without nightmares, woke up and made the third coffee of the seven-day supply. That was the first day in over a year that I heard myself laugh. I actually laughed. At a stupid little joke I thought in my head, but it was a laugh. Something playful, almost joyful.

I did my hair and put on some makeup and asked my husband to take me out. To actually take me out in public and see other human beings. I knew the change had something to do with that dang happy coffee. It was unbelievable. I mean, yeah, I kinda wanted to be able to go on Facebook and blast this woman's product—but I couldn't. It was working.

I kept drinking it. Everyday. One cup of happy coffee in the morning, and I was feeling better. Very quickly, people all around me began to notice a huge difference in my persona, in my lifeforce.

"Some new light has been turned on," they'd say to me. "You look great."

I lost 92 pounds. It just dropped off of me. I was walking more. I was moving my body. I was laughing and smiling and seeing the Yin in the Yang.

"I am alive," I said out loud one day. "I feel alive."

I started to enjoy life again. All, perhaps, because of some coffee that some crazy woman told me about. Such is the rollercoaster of life.

Chapter XV

Manifestation is Real

My son Jayden had always struggled with ADHD and behavior issues at school. After Shakiah had gone, they got increasingly worse. They got bad. I blamed it on the fact that in fourth grade Jayden collapsed on the football field and was diagnosed with prolonged QT: a heart condition in which his heart wasn't recharging enough for the next beat.

Translation: my very athletic, talented, strong child could no longer ride a bike, could no longer climb a tree, could no longer participate in gym class. And he could no longer take the ADHD medication he had been on since he was five. In the time after that diagnosis, my child went from a straight-A student, class-clown-tons-of-fun-kid to failing every spelling test and me getting near-daily phone calls from his teachers and counselors. He got suspended for "being uncontrollable."

"Enough is enough," I said to myself. "This coffee is working for me—is it safe for a child?"

I'd already become good friends with the formulator of the product, a nice, genius of a man named Kevin.

"Is it safe for a thirteen-year-old?" I asked him over the phone.

"It is. Give him half a serving—half a scoop—and see how he feels. Then go from there."

The next morning with his breakfast, Jayden got a half a scoop of the elixir. He said that he liked the taste. He packed his backpack and off he went to school.

Within a week, I got an email from his counselor at school: "Lindsey, what did you do? What did you do to this child to make him fun to be around? He's not talking back anymore. He's taking direction, and he's aced his last couple tests. What did you do?"

"I gave him some coffee?"

"Coffee?"

"Coffee—but not for the caffeine."

"I'm confused."

"It's special coffee," I said. "Happy coffee. Just trust me on this one."

"Alright. Whatever it is that you're doing, just keep it up."

"It's the coffee."

"Okay," said the voice on the other line, more than a hint of disbelief in its tone. "Just keep doing what you're doing."

I watched Jayden come out of his shell. Day by day, he woke up. Day by day, his smile came easier. Day by day, he became happier. I watched his panic attacks ease and then cease.

"Thanks mom," he said to me one day on our porch as we rocked in our chairs and felt the breeze on our faces. "I'm feeling a lot better now."

Jayden proceeded to lose 31 pounds. I realized that I hadn't taken any of my anxiety medication since I started my coffee routine. Our relationship was better than it had ever been. The horror film was fading, and the journey became almost beautiful.

My husband, however, wasn't a believer. Despite the obvious uplift in his wife and his son, he wouldn't drink his own. Refused. I'd find the cup I poured for him in the morning still on his bedside table at night and I'd have to throw it out.

"Why aren't you drinking your coffee?" I'd ask.

"Because you put that shit in it. I saw you."

Some people just can't see a miracle, even when it's put right in front of their eyes. But I visualized success. I visualized Ryan actually taking that first sip. I saw it happen in my mind. And then, he did.

Because manifestation is real.

Ryan eventually came around. It took a couple years, but he did. He couldn't see the miracle for what it was right away, but he also couldn't deny the differences he was observing in his wife and child. He started drinking his happy coffee and our relationship just kept improving. We really were the loves of each other's lives.

"Honey," I said to him over lunch one day a couple months ago, "what if we renew our vows?"

"Why babe?"

"Well, to be honest, with all the Xanax and booze that day, I really don't remember our wedding all that much. I'd like to have a fresh image."

"That sounds good, babe. Let's do it."

And so we are. Shortly after the publication of this book, my soulmate and I will renew our vows. I can't wait.

Chapter XVI

Coffee to the Rescue

Life was looking less dark. Almost bright even. I was working full time as a county appraiser here in Douglas County. It was a wonderful government job with amazing benefits. Great pay and a company car, too. We were still living paycheck to paycheck, but we felt taken care of. I felt taken care of. Jayden too.

When I first started using the coffee, it was costing me about $80 a month for a full supply for one person. In order to offset that cost, to be able to afford this life-changing cure—it felt like a *cure*—I decided that I would sign up to sell it and, if nothing else, at least get a discount on my personal orders. I'd dabbled in MLM companies before. Why not give it a try? Maybe I could even get a few friends or colleagues to see the benefits and start buying the product through me.

"Who knows," I thought. "Maybe I can at least cover the cost for Jayden and I?"

Well, the first month in the company I made $3,000. Second month? Seven thousand. And by just the third month of selling Happy Coffee, I was bringing in an extra $10,000 on top of my appraiser job. No joke.

*

Jayden's dentist had just told me he needed braces. If it weren't for this new income, we couldn't have afforded that $4K bill. If it weren't for Happy Coffee, Jayden would have crooked teeth. But you know what? His teeth are perfect.

My side-hustle with the coffee quickly proved to be my main stream of income. I floated the idea of quitting my appraiser job, but loyalty to the county and my co-workers kept me there. I was getting up at 4:30 in the morning: I'd work my Happy Coffee business for a couple hours then go work a full day at the office. On my lunch and during my fifteen-minute breaks, I was slinging coffee. Then I'd come home, cook dinner, and work until shortly before falling asleep. If I slept at all. But the lack of sleep wasn't because of nightmares anymore—it was because of excitement. It was because a zest for life had returned.

Or had I ever known it before?

I was running samples to the post office, to the café, to the guys at the firehouse. Anything to get this product into everybody's hands I could. I was hustling. I was movin' and shakin' to share something that had saved my life. Yeah, it was proving a good income stream for me but what ultimately pushed me was to help people.

In anything in business, it's so much better to work with a product you believe in. And I couldn't have believed in anything more. Not even if Gandalf himself had brewed his own cup of magic coffee or Jack had given me one of his famous beanstalk-sprouting beans. Not even if Paul Bunyan had ridden in on Babe the Blue Ox himself and handed me a nugget of gold. Nah, this coffee was better than all that. This coffee was an elixir of life, a fountain of youth, a spring-loaded pathway forward into a life worth living.

I knew if it could save my life that I could save hundreds of people's lives with it. For perhaps the first time in my life I didn't feel guilty. I didn't feel like I was letting someone down. I didn't feel like the one who couldn't save her parents' marriage or her uncle or her cousin's life. I didn't feel like the mother who couldn't save Shakiah. I felt like a human who had a purpose—a strong and positive and therapeutic purpose. I could change the world. And I was.

I was helping human beings crawl out of the depths of darkness, depression and despair—with a cup of coffee. It became my avocation. The old lady in line at the Goodwill? She was about to hear about Happy Coffee. The cashier at the restaurant? Her too.

And by October of that year, my business was flourishing. I was in the top 2% of the company. I was bringing in nearly $20,000 a month. And, at least for a while, I was truly happy.

*

Then came October. Time for the trial of the man who murdered Shakiah. It had come out that the fire was arson. Someone had wanted to get back at Shakiah's grandmother and he'd murdered my daughter in the process. If it hadn't been for the coffee, I know I would have fallen back into the darkness. But I didn't. I had some trouble focusing, and I was seeing therapists, but I was doing okay.

"I really think you need to take a step back," the therapist said from her chair one day as I lay sprawled on the couch. "You need to take some time off of work. You have gone through more than most people will go through in 20 lifetimes. How long has it been since you lost your daughter?"

"Six months."

"Yeah, and you haven't taken a day off a single day of work."

On some level, she was right. There were days when I was sleeping at my desk. I was burning the candle at both ends of both jobs to stay busy. To keep my mind occupied. To not let it stray back into the nightmares. I had screwed up some calculations. I was making errors. I was fighting my boss at the county job.

I agreed with my therapist and went in to talk to my boss about getting some time off so I could go to the trial.

"Well," she said, "I'd like you to be able to go to the trial, too, but you don't have any PTO left."

What a fucking cunt. I no longer cared. My life was about *my* life. "I'll see you next Tuesday," I said.

Sometimes it's better to ask for forgiveness rather than permission.

And it worked. All of my co-workers pooled together their PTO and vacation time and went to my boss. "We're giving them to Lindsey," they told her. "She needs to be at the trial."

My boss nixed it: "The policy states that these are non-transferrable and must be used only in cases of severe health or sick-leave issues."

Well, my therapist honed in on that real fast. She wrote a big fat letter that said something along the lines of, "Absolutely Lindsey is not capable of working right now due to this 'this and this.' She needs immediate family leave."

And so we applied for the Family Medical Leave Act. It was granted. Even if I couldn't get paid time off, I could leave unpaid and still keep my job. I could go to the trial and come back when I was ready. I stood up for myself. My friends came to my aid. My therapist too. I had a team behind me. And I was leading the charge.

Photo Captured on my Drive to the Murder Trial. I had angels with me even then!

Ryan and I had started drifting apart. He was drinking a lot. And by a lot I mean like 18-24 beers a night. Every night. He was never a violent drunk, but it was taking its toll. He was far from present. He had numbed himself, was numbing himself, so much. Plus, even though I was making good money, we had expenses. And his drinking wasn't cheap. On any level.

It was then that I learned that network marketing is the number two work-related avenue for divorce. Real Estate is first, I suppose because you're such a slave to the phone, but network marketing is second. What? Yeah, I think it's just because you're in the fast lane so much. Always pushing to try to separate yourself.

Here I was, quickly at the top of my company, traveling extensively, gone somewhere every month, and I was finding a new side of me that I hadn't seen in years. I was loving life, but Ryan was at home taking care of the kids now. He didn't like it. He didn't like seeing his wife bringing in so much more money than he was. I was out living my life and going to meetings and doing all these things, and somewhere on the line our relationship started to go awry. The drinking got worse.

"Mommy," my daughter Jhetta said to me one day, "I really want to go to the gas station but it's after three o'clock so dad's too drunk to take me."

That stopped me in my place. Even at ten years old, Jhetta could identify that her dad was inebriated to a point where driving with him was not safe. At three o'clock in the afternoon no less.

But I didn't want to give up on my husband. Even though I could see the writing on the wall, some attachment issues from my childhood were making me stick around. Keeping me quiet. Keeping me covering up situations with band-aids when I knew they needed surgery.

For the first time in my life I didn't have to rely on a man to help pay my bills. I could do it all on my own. I still had trauma, but I had this growing belief that I didn't need anybody but myself. I could do it for my children. I *needed* to do it for my children.

"Ryan," I said that night after dinner. "I'm done. I'm going to the trial and when I get back we need to talk more."

The trial was about five hours away in Albion, so I packed my bags and set out. I would see justice done for my daughter.

The trial was a flood of emotions, and just looking at the man made the hairs stick up on the back of my neck. I went every day, sat in the same seat, and watched the process unfold. It wasn't easy. After eight days, justice was served, and he was found guilty for the murders of Paige and Shakiah. He was sentenced to life. For taking the life of my daughter.

I hadn't spoken to Ryan much while I was away. I needed the space, and he probably did too. When I returned home, I noticed his belly had shrunk. He almost looked skinny.

"Mommy!" Jhetta said as she wrapped me in a hug. "Daddy hasn't had a drink since you've been gone!"

I was awestruck. Later that evening I went up to Ryan. "This isn't the first time I've asked you to put down the booze," I said. "What changed?"

"It's the coffee," said Ryan, apology thick on his tongue. "I started drinking it."

"You did?"

"Yeah, and I have no desire to drink beer."

First, the product saved my life. Then Jayden's. And now it looked like it had just saved my marriage.

*

December showed up. I had just come back to work from being on family medical leave. Straight off, I got pulled into the office and I'm basically being asked pointed questions by my employer, who has been completely stalking my Facebook. She saw that I had got into a car accident, wrecked my car and had to get a new one. She literally tried to use it against me: that I bought a new vehicle while on family medical so, clearly, I was "in the right mind and should have been working."

What? It was a whole hot-mess disaster, and that night my husband just said, "quit that fucking job. You don't need it."

So I did. I was making ten grand a month with the coffee. Ten thousand dollars a month. I put my resignation in at the county and quit an appraiser job that most 34-year-olds in the Midwest would dream of having. In my own way I was saying, "No fucking way someone is going to be in control of my life."

It was time that my feelings came first. Plus, I felt like I could finally afford it—in more ways than one.

Chapter XVII

If It Ain't Broke, Don't Fix It

      Things were working again. By February of 2019, I'd taken my team at what we now call 'The Practice Company' to Ambassador, a level where we were bringing in over $300K a month in sales. It was incredible, like, what the hell, like I'm not even working hard enough to make 20 grand?

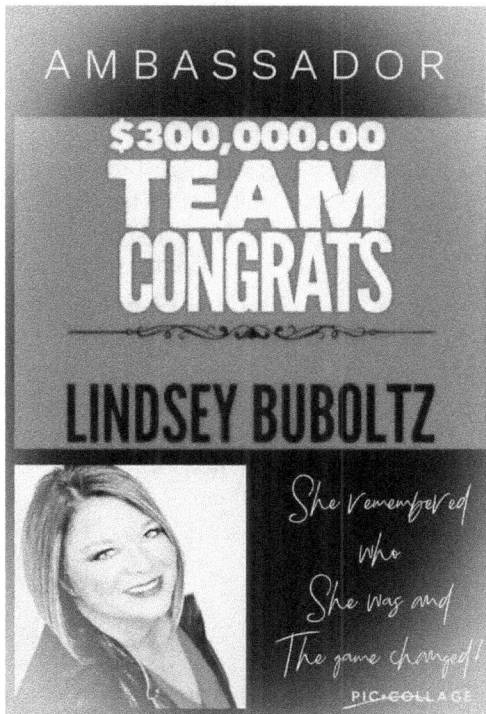

AMBASSADOR

$300,000.00

TEAM CONGRATS

LINDSEY BUBOLTZ

She remembered who She was and The game changed!

PIC·COLLAGE

      And that was the biggest mistake I probably ever made, putting that out into the universe and saying out loud that I was not worthy of my income.

Because it wasn't much longer after those words that the folks with the happy coffee went and changed up a great thing. They messed with the formula, trying to 'perfect it.' What? It *was* perfected. What the hell were they thinking?

I tried to stop it but it happened anyway. The FDA had come in and said that one of our ingredients wasn't safe and the formulation had to change. The happy coffee formulation no longer worked. For me and for a lot of people. I was quickly back on my anxiety-depression medication. I gained weight. Jayden was the same on both. From January to December of that year, I spent thousands of dollars at the doctor trying to figure out what the hell was wrong with me.

They'd changed the formula, and the formula of my life had stopped balancing. I got tested for everything. All the mental stuff, the acid reflux, maybe some major gastrointestinal issue thing. My hair was falling out by the handfuls. I had no energy. I mean, we tested for anything and everything.

My business continued to crumble around me, and before I knew it, come December of this year my paycheck had dwindled to a fraction of what I had been making. I couldn't pay the bills. Couldn't pay my business bills let alone my family's bills. I had no clue what I was going to do.

"I think I'm just gonna get a job at like Omaha Steaks or something for the winter," I told Ryan.

"Grandma and grandpa told you the coffee income wasn't gonna last," Jayden reminded me. "That *was* a good job at the county."

I was down. Down but not out. I needed something new. And so I created it. I made it happen.

Let me give you one of life's greatest lessons—no matter how many times you get knocked down, you can always get back up. And you can always make it better. On the opposite side of fear is fantastic.

So I crossed to the other side.

On December 15th of 2020, I resigned from The Practice Company. The product was no longer helping people, so I walked away with no back up plan. Well, a $14/hour backup plan. I worked at Omaha Steaks through the holiday and put some cash in my pocket and made sure the kids had Christmas. Then I launched with AmpLIFEi—a new company that the original founder of The Practice Company had just started. I began taking their trial product. It worked. It worked like the old one. The formulator had replaced the ingredient that the FDA had nixed with a formulation of all-natural ingredients. That genius! He did it. The elixir was back.

After nine months of joint pain, inability to walk, anxiety and depression returning, hair falling out, a diagnosis of a pituitary gland tumor, a fear of cancer in my brain, and all of these things going on, I started on the new product. Lo and behold, my joints stopped hurting. I lost a quick 12 pounds and my hair stopped falling out. I was sleeping through the night, no longer sleepwalking through the day. I was me. I was back.

"It was leaky gut all along," I heard from the doctor one day. AmpLIFEi coffee was working. It was working for me, and I was ready to reach others and have it work for them.

*

The docs had tested me for celiac and autoimmune and all those other things for the gut because I had every one of those symptoms. The 'before and afters' I posted on Facebook blew up. Something like 3,500 views and they wanted their hands on what I had mine on. Les Brown put out a quote saying something like, "if she left The Practice Company, whatever she's found must be damn good."

Eighty-five percent of my team chose to follow me to AmpLIFEi. (Interesting stuff there, and we'll get back to that.)

Before I made the decision to leave, I'd gone to my upline and I told her, "I can't pay my bills. I cannot continue here—the product isn't working. I can't sell something that's not helping people."

"I'm sorry to hear that."

"Yeah, and I'm not so sure that the new formulation hasn't been what's making me sick for the last nine months. I know it will affect the bottom line and so out of respect for you, I just want you to know I'm not sure how much longer I'm gonna stay here."

"Stick it out for a week," she said, almost pleadingly. "Just give me a week to sort some things out."

They had changed the formula and a product that was saving people's lives was now failing them. By the hundreds, people had stopped receiving the benefits. If they had been depressed before, they were again. If their joints had been pain-free for a while, the hurting recommenced.

I heard the same storm every single time. "It's just not working anymore. I'm back on my meds. The panic attacks have come back and I'm gaining weight."

That's why I went to AmpLIFEi.

My paycheck for the first two weeks at AmpLIFEi was over $12,000. Then it was twenty grand a month. Then $40,000. And I'd only been here three months! We grew into the third team in the company to go to a half a million dollars. We we're on pace to be the third team in the company to hit a million dollars. And the only other person in the company that's done that is my upline, so half of her volume was mine.

Things were going great. But to get to this place I had to get some coaching. Let me fill you in on that story.

Chapter XVIII

Seagulls and Sharks

Like I told you, at the end of my time with The Practice Company and before I made the move to AmpLIFEi, I had gone back on my anxiety meds. I hated swallowing handfuls of pills at a time. I knew I needed something else. That something else was meeting a coach and starting to work with her. It changed my life.

It was September 2019 and I was attending our monthly women's network meeting with eWomen Network. It was a live event, and we were doing our standard roundtable brainstorm discussion and I was like, "We need to branch out and market into Canada." And so I put this out in the universe at the beginning of the meeting, and then they brought on the presenter for the day.

I listened to her speak. My first impression of her was that she was kind of a bitch. (But she's one of my dearest friends now, and we laugh about it to this day.) But, yeah, I didn't like her 'pitch' and I thought she was a bit of a bitch.

Her name was Michele Gundersen, and she was a storytelling expert. My first impression of her was not favorable. I didn't like her pitch and I thought she was kind of a bitch. But then, the more she spoke, the more I came around to what she was saying. She made sense and I totally came around to what she was saying about 'story'—so much so that I signed up for her strategy session.

Then, at the end of presentation and before that strategy session, she held a drawing to give away a free ticket to her 'Story Freedom' retreats set to take place in Banff, Alberta, Canada.

I'm like, "Yeah, I could do this." I had already been thinking about Canada all day and I really put my intention out. Put it out strongly to the universe that this trip to Canada and a storytelling course is in line with what I'm thinking.

And, of course, my ticket was drawn.

"Okay, Universe," I said to myself, "you're hearing me and I'm hearing you. Let's go to Canada. Let's do this."

I'd just won a high-ticket item. And I was going to cash in. But first, Michele and I did our 'strategy session' together. I was blown away. We were supposed to have 30 minutes together, but it turned into a three-and-a-half-hour strategy *awakening*. What was masked as a 'storytelling marketing session' became this, like, healing-intensive therapy-thing. Michele gave me more healing than I'd received in three *years* of energy work. We talked about childhood and how things that have happened to us still show up in our stories today. We spoke about regression and implementation and maybe even touched on transmigration of the soul.

"Who *is* this woman?" I thought.

A couple months later, I flew to Banff to continue my work with her. It was so beautiful—Rocky Mountains and teal waters and god's majesty. The pictures I'd seen beforehand didn't even do it justice. It was gorgeous. And the conference itself was beyond amazing.

We picked up where we left off in that three-and-a-half-hour strategy session. She was helping me tell my story by learning about my story—by helping *me* learn about my story. As obvious as it seems, I had had a rough one and those hurts were still manifesting themselves in my life. Were still manifesting themselves in my storytelling, the stories I told about myself and how they related to the products I was selling.

Michele was a muse. She was like this ancient storytelling wizard living in modern times. She drew on historical principles, singular truths, aspects to hit on in a story that make it universal and easily absorbed by an audience.

From that first virtual meeting through the strategy session and into the retreat in Banff, Michele became my mentor. I had always wanted to write a book but would get a few pages in and then shelve it for a year. I'd start and stop only to start and stop again. I could never get everything out. But after the session with this storyteller, we made progress with my story, and it felt like a huge weight had just been lifted from my shoulders. I was just like, "Whoa, what was *that* about?"

The event in Canada went on for three days, and I still can't do it justice with a description. It was almost like this 'elsewhere' feeling. Beyond body or something: spirit channeling maybe.

I cried, I laughed, I worked through a lot. We did a lot of activities, and I met the other attendees. We all grew a lot in that short time.

I know I did.

Then, at the end of the course, Michele hit us with her upsell—what we could do next to take our growth to the next level. She had her coaching program, three levels of time and money and benefits. Since my awakening in that first three-and-a-half-hour session, I'd been yearning to continue my work with her, but I hadn't made up my mind which one I was going to choose.

We were in the middle of a session on the last day, and I got this download. It came from me but was also not from me. It electrified me. I stood up. Jumped up, really. And in front of the whole room, I shouted out with shock and joy in my voice: "Diamond Elite. I'm going Diamond Elite!"

The room went quiet. Silent and stone. 'Diamond Elite' was a $65,000 investment.

"Whoa," said one of my cohorts.

"Holy shit," mouthed another.

I'd proclaimed my intent. Now I had to follow through on it. Despite the almost instant feeling of cold feet, I had to do it. I *would* do it.

The session ended, and we all began milling about. I found my friend Beth in the hallway and with wide eyes I said, "Fuck! $65,000, what was I thinking?"

"Lindsey, relax, you're making $25,000 a month. You can afford it."

"You think I should do it?"

"You've spent a lot of money on a lot of other things in your life. How much have you spent on therapists in the last three years alone?"

I saw her point. It was an investment in myself. If that first three-and-a-half hours was the best thing since sliced bread, imagine what return I would get on 65K and an entire year of illumination.

"You're right," I said to Beth. "This is my opportunity to see healing in real time."

And so I embarked on that journey with Michele. I embarked on the journey with my 'story freedom.' It was a whirlwind, full of ups and downs and all arounds. I learned my story. I learned how to process it and how to use it. I learned that, though my story had been a difficult one, one filled with pain, that 'I had lived it'—and there was strength in that. I had a story worth telling.

We worked intensively together. Michele was drawing stories out of me left and right. We went down to Mexico right before the Corona-thing hit, and we spent seven days in a little villa together as pupil and teacher. Every morning, I would get up early and go down to the little restaurant-café. I would chat with the baristas as I ordered my coffee and then I would go down to the beach where I would sit with crossed legs and watch the sun come up. Michele would wake up a little after me and do her yoga on the patio. When the sun was up, I'd return, and we would do our morning session together.

"How was your sunrise time?" she asked me

"You know, I was watching the seagulls fly, these beautiful agile seagulls just flying over the ocean—but in my mind all I could envision was a shark breaching the water and eating the seagull."

"How did it make you feel?"

"Anxious. I couldn't relax—all I could think about was, at any moment, a predator was going to come out of the water and eat these seagulls."

It was the metaphor for my life! When things looked good, when things looked beautiful or happy or free, that is always when the bottom dropped out. It's how it happened in my life, it's how I've portrayed it in this book, but until that morning thinking about seagulls and sharks, it had never occurred to me. I'd never seen it.

"We can be so blind to our own lives," Michele said. "Even though we see others' lives so easily, we often simply do not see our own path with nearly as much clarity."

The private coaching week in Mexico continued on. We made sticky notes and vision boards for my life, sticky notes and vision boards that are and always will be present in my office. Upon the walls where I can see their truths loud and proud.

And we even had one 'free day.' We ventured out into Cabo, and we were going to do "whatever we wanted." We went to a nice lunch at a quaint little café, and then we bopped around downtown Cabo and literally ran into a storefront for a whale watching tour.

"Yes!" I shouted into the sky, "this is what I want to do. I want to go on a whale watching tour."

"It's your day, Lindsey."

So we get in this tiny little glass-bottom boat. "Oh my God," I said as I climbed aboard onto the little boat to go out into the middle of the ocean. (We're not talking about some ocean liner here, we're talking a little dinghy type thing. And the waves weren't small.)

But through the glass-bottom we're seeing fish in all their multicolored gorgeousness and we're keeping a look out for whales. A huge flock of seagulls showed up overhead and came to rest on the water in front of us.

"Birds usually lead the way," said the captain.

And, then, there it was. Like magic—a perfect humpback whale breached right out of the blue waters before me. It was majestic, ancient, timeless, perfect. Then another. And another.

"Wow," I said, tears of awe and joy in my eyes. "Wow."

And no seagulls got eaten. Not one. The birds and the fish and the humpbacks all co-mingled in the sea and did their primordial thing. There was balance. There was flow. It worked.

And I had a vision, for myself, for moving forward with my life.

With Michele Gunderson, my teacher

Chapter XIX

The Universe is Listening

So I completed my year with Michele and I learned a lot and I grew as a human being—but, despite it all, my business with The Practice Company was starting to crumble. And my health was not good. Going the wrong way. As the year went on, I was physically unable to show up for many of our sessions. I started to feel like I wasted all of this money. It became difficult to make the payments. They started going on my credit card. (Not a good thing.) But we were set to do another trip to Mexico, and I was really looking forward to it. Then the Coronavirus thing hit. Then the Coronavirus *World* descended upon us. The Mexico trip became 'virtual.' What? You can't do a beach virtually. I'm sorry. But you can't. You just can't.

So I changed my perspective. I had to. And, in one very real aspect, that first (and only) trip to Mexico became, to me, worth the $65K. Expensive vacation, I know—but the moment of awakening was priceless. It was probably worth a million dollars. Because in the moments of those days I discovered how all the ties in my story were holding me back.

One of the real tangible 'ahas' was about manifestation. Like when I said, out loud, that I wasn't worthy of making $20,000 a month. Yeah, well the universe heard that.

We all speak a language with the universe. It's as old as time. And it's two-way communication for sure. We have to see the signs, and we have to give off intention. So, it was time to start thinking abundantly—that much was certain.

So now I do spend a lot of my time in abundance, in the realm of abundance where I allow good things to come. Where I *know* good things will come. Because they do. It's almost crazy to think, but they do.

*

I remember when my dad won the lottery when I was in middle school. The ticket that got us to Guthrie Center and a new life. I thought it was too good to be true. I think my whole family did. And, though it bought us a house and some fun toys, we weren't ready for things to be great and amazing—we weren't ready to live in the abundance— and that golden ticket crushed down on us and literally ruined our family and took my stepdad away from me. And we all manifested it. Individually and collectively.

That experience came to make me see money as an evil. I saw the influx of money and the negativity that surrounded it, and I adopted that mindset. And it stayed with me. Whether you had it or you didn't, this thing called money was 'evil.' Whether you were floating on top of the clouds with lottery money or living paycheck-to-paycheck and struggling to pay the bills, money was a *problem*. The mantra-mindset stayed with me—and so it became so.

That was the underlying force of my business declining so rapidly after I said those words out loud. I was given this beautiful abundance of business and income-flow, and I didn't feel worthy of it. But, because of my time with Michele in Mexico, because of my lesson on the beach with whales and seagulls, I finally realized that I *am* worthy. That I can live in abundance.

And, as I write this book, dear reader, I can say without any drip of hesitation, that I am abundant. That my life is abundant. And with a little change of mindset, yours can be too. Give it a try. Think abundantly—and see what comes.

"Think abundantly, and see what comes…"

Chapter XX

On Stage

So, May of 2019, I went to this event and as the top seller and leader in The Practice Company. I was given a prime time speaking spot. I was to share my (heart wrenching) testimonial about my experience with the product. I was asked to speak from the stage and share my story.

I remember driving there that morning and arriving at the event's center—and there he is, there is 'the man.' There is Les Brown. The former congressman and bestselling author, and the motivational speaker I've listened to every morning for years; he's at the door, greeting people. He's someone I had looked up to, in awe, and someone I never imagined would be right in front of me. Someone I never thought would shake my hand. Someone I never thought would give me a hug. Never Someone I never thought would look me in the eye and say with a million-dollar smile, "Lindsey, you smell like fresh money."

I blushed like something redder than a tomato and walked to my table and sat down thinking *how the hell does Les Brown know my name—and what does he mean 'I smell like fresh money?'*

I wasn't sure, but I liked it and I took it. I sat at my table and talked with some kind folks, and the event went on with its speakers and presentations. A little later, it was my turn to speak. I was brought up on stage to share my story. I spoke from the heart. I told my story. The audience picked up what I threw down. The ovation was a loud one, and I felt great.

As I walked off stage, Les Brown was right there in front of me. He grabbed my hands, and he looked into my soul through my eyes. "You belong on that stage," he said. "That's where you belong."

I couldn't believe it.

That was the first time I had been on stage as a motivational speaker. It wouldn't be the last. I've grown to love the stage. In regular life I don't seek out attention, but I have grown to love being up on the stage, this little introvert up on stage in front of thousands of people at a time, crushing it. Audiences, human beings, not feeling sorry for me because of my story but feeling inspired *by* me because of my story.

I have this to say about speaking: We humans respond to emotions, to pathos, to what tugs at the strings of our heart. Don't read from a script. Speak from your heart. If you want to move an audience, speak from your heart straight into theirs.

Chapter XXI

I'm on a Magazine?

My magazine came. The one with the article about me. What?! It was so cool. I had made Ambassador with The Practice Company and they were putting me on the cover. A full cover story. On me. It was very cool. I felt like a rock star. People started asking for signed copies.

I signed a bunch. But, in the moment of talking with an individual and thinking of something witty to write on the magazine to accompany my signature, I had trouble coming up with the right words. So, one day, I just went through the few dozen I still had on hand and signed them with a few quotes that I'd always loved: inspirational quotes, you know, quotes to live by.

And then when someone asked for one, I'd pull one out, letting my intuition guide me, and hand it to them or mail it to them. I went purely on feel. Feeling which quote was right for them. And literally every time someone has received one, they've been like, "Lindsey, OMG, thank you for the signed magazine—that quote you put on there was exactly what I needed!"

Every time.

As I'm writing this, I just pulled a magazine from my computer bag. Let's see what this one says:

Let everyone who crosses your path leave happier.

Wow, that one works. It works for me right now. In this moment. It speaks to me, and maybe it even does to you. Because remember this: no matter what we do, it's how we do it. And it's all about interactions.

Money is about relationships. Happiness is about relationships. (Especially the relationship with yourself.) If everyone who crosses your path leaves happier than when they entered, they will remember you. Fondly.

We only get one chance at a first impression—and that impression is how people will remember you. It tinges how future interactions will go. It shapes how the words you tell people will be absorbed and received.

And I always try to impart something good to people. No matter if it's the barista you order your latte from or the person at the toll booth or a future client. Treating every interaction in that moment as 'the most important thing in your life' will leave a lasting impression. And always remember, the thing you are doing right now *is* the most important thing in your life. Life is made up of a series of 'right now's.' Your big business meeting tomorrow is not more important than enjoying, fully, your glass of coffee or orange juice, today.

Tomorrow will come. Yesterday has already happened. Today is the gift. And in every human interaction you have, you have the opportunity to improve the life of another person. If you do that often enough, it becomes your flow—and that is powerful. That is power. And that is how you will be viewed. That is how you will be absorbed and remembered. Both in-person and online.

I say that "your Facebook presence is a multi-million-dollar brand." How you present yourself is your brand. Whether it's in a seemingly small interaction with someone you don't know or it's your brand marketing online, do it to the apex of potential. Because potential leads to action. And action leads to good things.

There's a lot of really shitty MLM marketing for people that are just starting out, and I always strive to be different—to put in the time to make whatever I am doing stand out. I'd encourage you to do the same. Some of my peers and competitors just don't give the care that they need to take their business (and life) to the next level. But it is all within our control. We can make it or break it all by ourselves. Work, dear reader, to be engaging.

I engage with people in person *and* online. All the time, and with all I am.

I ask them questions. I comment on their posts. I create a two-way conversation. I *engage*—I give to receive, and then I sit back and allow the good flood to come, sending them to my link to sign up. It's positive. It's honest. It's real. I truly believe in what I am doing, and people pick up on the energy.

Never do anything half-ass. People can smell a fake. People respect, and show up for, the real thing.

If I do nothing else in my life, I will be real. And I think you should be too. It's a good way to walk.

Chapter XXII

Fork in the Road

So, the owner of AmpLIFEi was the original founder of The Practice Company, a man named Robert. It's not really my story to tell, but I will say this: that company was, in the opinion of some, stolen from Robert by the corporate executives he brought in to help him. They came in and wormed their way to basically taking the company out from under him. The details are gory, and there are enough of those already in this book, so I'll spare you.

In short, Robert said, "fuck it" and launched a new company. Started it all over from the ground floor. He's the guru. He's the genius. But the damn FDA blacklisted one little ingredient in his formula—and that's why he had to reformulate.

I learned from this. I knew the product was safe. I had been using it every day for years. My body and my mind and my soul knows a lot more than some white-coat lab resident at the FDA. Marijuana used to be illegal, right? Now in almost half the country it ain't, and it continues to gain acceptance every election.

So I'll tell you what I've done.

Because I know my body better than the government does, I've created a stockpile. The 'cache of all caches.' If some pencil pusher wants to take my elixir from me again, I'm good: I've been ordering twenty extra tubs every month for a while now. Through my own research I know the product's shelf-life is beyond amazing; for up to five years after the expiration date, it's good. Five years!

And don't get squeamish here, but I also know this: Even if a little bit of mold sneaks in there after a few years, I can still boil it in 180 degree-plus water and kill the mold—and it's good as new. Yep. Magic, this stuff.

How did I learn this? Well, how did the first person ever eat an artichoke? She tried it.

When the reformulation came about and I ran out of the original product, I started feeling bad again. (Duh.) But I got a call from a downline reseller who was resigning from the business. I asked her if she had any product.

"Uh, yeah, I have like eight tubs but they're all expired."

"Don't you dare throw that stuff away!" I shot into the phone.

"Huh?"

"I'm coming over. I'm getting in the car right now—I'll buy it off you at full price."

I drove the hour-and-a-half drive in like 67 minutes. I paid her for six months-worth of the original blend of the coffee. Most of it was as good as the day it was brewed, and with the rest I boiled away the small amount of mold. It worked. It was safe. It continued to save my life.

It was right then that I knew I would travel the earth to hunt down whoever had any of it left—and my stockpile began to grow. I've even purchased an open tub at a garage sale. Yep. That's me. That's how salvational this product is.

*

So, at this point you may be thinking, "what the heck is in this coffee that makes it so wonderful?"

Well, the genius is in the synthesis, in how it's combined and activated. You couldn't just get the list of ingredients and ingest them individually. It's like how coal is really the same stuff as diamonds. They're made of the same thing, except that the diamonds have been, like, super, super, highly pressurized—and that changes what it is. Same with the coffee, it's how it is all combined and activated when ingested by the body as a single, perfect, flowing entity. It's in the gut/brain process, and the perfect absorption of the product by the body.

*

Most Americans suffer with some sort of gut-health issue. So, if you're ingesting a supplement or whatever that can only be ingested by the gut, there's going to be absorption issues—it's not efficient and, in many cases, simply can't be taken, it just gets flushed out into the toilet. Not true for my magic coffee: because of its unique formulation, it has the ability to be absorbed from the moment it hits your lips, through your mouth, then as it trickles down your throat the esophagus can absorb it; as it gets into your stomach, the small intestines get *their* share—all of this highly efficient science bringing it straight to your brain where it kick-starts your gut-brain connection.

And it's balanced. It tells our brain that we don't need to overeat or overdrink to get our dopamine rush. We aren't experiencing unnecessary pain because now that we've got the brain firing on all neurotransmitter-levels, so we don't need the daily ibuprofen or Tylenol or painkillers. We've boosted the serotonin which turns to the melatonin that gifts us rejuvenating, through-the-night rest.

And, I mean, it *is* coffee—so it does have some caffeine (less than a cup at Starbucks) and other natural energy elements to it as well. So no need for the Red Bull or Five Hour Energy after Five Hour Energy.

Anywho, I'm more of an intuit than a scientist, and when a client asks me about the product, I'll just tell them how it has benefited my life—and how, if they try it for even just a day or two, it will be theirs as well.

Oh, and I've become great friends with the formulator, and he knows that I am prepared to take out a bank loan to pay him millions of dollars to make it, just for me, if it ever disappears again.

Kevin Thomas, Formulator and my favorite Mad Scientist.

Chapter XXIII

Me and the Gator

I'd just won my first trip from my upline. We were headed to Florida! To Orange Beach, Florida, and I was jazzed.

I packed my bags and flew south, ready for adventure and good times. We were set for a day of tubing down the Black River.

I hesitated. "Wait. . . it's Florida. . . what about alligators?"

"Ah, don't be a wimp, Lindsey!"

I'd won the trip. I *had* to follow through. Gators or not. We loaded the bus and drove through the woods to the water's edge.

"But, seriously," I asked the bus driver. "Are there gators in these waters?"

He smiled a little grin. "Just keep your toes out of the water—and get out of the river before six."

"Why 'six?'"

"Cuz that's gator feeding time."

I was scared shitless.

But I got in my innertube and started floating down the river. I couldn't let the girls see my squeamishness.

"Watch out for the gators!" they kept yelling to me around every bend in the river.

After a few drinks, my apprehension calmed. The summer sun beat down on my skin and we floated for hours, just talking and laughing and being grown up girls.

We came around another bend. It was dark in the shade from the trees. I saw two large eyes.

"That gator ain't got nothin' on me!" I screamed with a little help from the booze.

I kicked and swam toward the alligator. Me and an alligator in the Black River of Florida. Closer I got. Closer. And then, I started wrestling with it.

I'm not sure what the other women thought. A mother and her two little boys were screaming their heads off. "What are you doing?!" they called.

I giggled and splashed around with the gator—the biggest, most life-like inflatable alligator I'd ever seen.

For the rest of the trip, I was known simply as 'Gator.' And the next conference when I went up on stage to receive my sales award, I did so inside a blow-up alligator costume. In front of thousands of people. And they were all laughing. It was a beautiful sound.

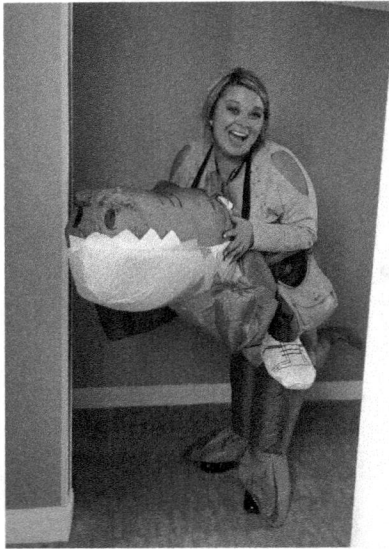

I love working in a career that allows me to travel with the men and women I love most in the world.

Chapter XXIV

A Kitten and Steven and Soul, Oh My

I don't know how I ended up at a farm just outside of Panora, Iowa just after Carrie's memorial where this little baby kitten was living, but I did. I'd just lost my best friend Carrie, and I happened to be on a farm when a life was brought into the world. Sometimes, that is how things work. Actually, oftentimes, that is how things work. I'd lost Carrie, and I found Gauge. One door closes and another opens.

It's for this reason that the Ying-Yang symbol has been a best-seller for a long time now. It jives with people. Has been for thousands of years. And that's because where there is life there is death—and where there is death, there is life. Balance. The Yin and the Yang.

*

Let's go to another conference: Let's go to March 2021 in Indianapolis. Because at that conference there was another crazy thing happening in my life—a young man, new to my team, and he had no money to get there. He was this eager and passionate old kid, and he just didn't have the funds to make the trip.

But we all wanted him to be there. I'm pretty sure we all asked the universe to make it happen. And it did.

We got him a ride, and his upline bought him some nice clothes he could wear. She even allowed him to sleep on a cot in their hotel room. Just so he could come. And there was something so beautiful about this young man. I was drawn to him instantly.

I saw his aura and felt his energy and said to myself, "I'm going to make him a rock star in this business. I am." I mean, I want this for everyone on my team, but there was just something special about this human being. Steven, Steven was his name. And everywhere I went that weekend, I kept hearing his name. "Steven this... Steven that... Oh, yeah, that Steven—he's got somethin'."

And then this happened...

On the Sunday of that conference weekend, I woke up ready to live a great day. I put on Shakiah's necklace, the necklace I always wear during conferences because I truly believe my business is, in its way, a sort of pathway for her rebirth—like, even though she's gone, she's looking down on me from above and cheering me on, pushing me forward. I feel her energy. I feel her driving me forward. It's pretty spiritual.

And, back to this Sunday: Steven and I were leaving the conference together. We were walking out the front door side-by-side—and I figured it out. I figured out why I was so drawn to this kid. It was his eyes. They were almost identical to Shakiah's. They had the same essence, the same archetype.

At that time I didn't even know that much about Steven; I'd only heard a few of his stories. He'd lived a tough life, that much was certain, but he had this inner joy, this resonance of fearlessness. And when he spoke, the entire room lit up. He could make people laugh. He could make people cry. He had the gift. And it came from that inner well of resolve—what you could see when you looked into his eyes. People loved him. Just like Shakiah. Both so beautiful. They were made from the same stuff. Kind of like Carrie and Gauge.

*

Every time something or someone comes and knocks me down, it's people like Steven who help me get

124

back up. I feel great now. I've felt great for a long time. I didn't think life could keep getting better, but it does. Like, I'm serious, every time something shitty happens something else 10x better comes along right after it. I'm thinking, "Life is fantastic. I'm no longer thinking about the shark coming out of the water. I'm thinking about how many more seagulls are going to be flying with me in the future."

It took me 37 years to figure this thing out. That life is a rollercoaster, yes, but that life is also an ascension. We go through our days and months and years with downs and ups—yet the ups can keep getting higher while the lows no longer hit rock bottom.

Rock bottom. Maybe you've been there. Maybe you *are* there. I know I've been there, but as long as we work to find a purpose—whatever it is—the universe will work with us. Boldness is rewarded. I know when I kicked my addictions of food and constantly thinking about suicide, I was rewarded. You will be too.

My passion was, and is, for people. Helping people is my purpose, and helping people is what is making my highs so high right now. Natural highs. The good stuff. I love what I do. People send me messages all the time about how I have helped their health or their financial trajectory or even just their self-confidence. And, actually, I shouldn't even write the 'just' in that sentence. Self-confidence is huge. Belief in yourself is huge.

So, start believing. You'll be amazed at what you find.

Chapter XXV

My Friend, Kat

Kathleen Smith. Her name is Kathleen Smith, and she is a rock star's rock star. She's been a pillar for me for a long time. And it was crazy how we met.

It was a month after Shakiah's death. I was at Norwex at the time, the cleaning supplies company. We had another convention, and I was feeling like it was time to do something. Time to try, at least in the slightest, to get back to my normal routine. So I packed my bag and off I went bound for Minneapolis. I was just going to try to have the best time that I could.

"I'm going to focus on the business," I told myself. "I'm going to get back into the swing of life."

Well, then some more Life happened. We'd all gone out and had some fun after day two of the conference, and I found myself sitting on a park bench with Kat, this woman I'd just met. We hit it off. We told silly stories and laughed, and we told serious stories and cried. We felt immediate, intimate trust with one another. It was very cool.

And then we heard this blood curdling scream.

Two-thirty in the morning and we're sitting on a park bench just outside the hotel, and we hear this sound. A human, in pain. My instinct kicked in, and I started running toward the screaming. Kathleen followed me. It wasn't too far away, and we rounded a corner and there was this young girl, who couldn't be more than twenty—she's crying, half her clothes are missing. She's a heap of misfortune, probably drugged and likely assaulted.

"Are you alright?" I called to her. It was obvious she wasn't.

I walked up to her and put my arms around her. I just held her and let her cry. I didn't ask too many questions, but it was obvious that something wasn't right. She hinted that she had been sex trafficked. We called the police and the paramedics. We tried to get the story out of her, at least get her name, but she wouldn't talk much. Maybe she *couldn't* talk. She just buried her head in my shoulders and held me tight.

The ambulance was there in no time, and the paramedics were trying to get her inside, trying to take her.

"Don't leave me," the little girl said to me as tears flooded from her bloodshot eyes.

I looked at the paramedics, and I looked back to the girl's face. I didn't know what to do. She grabbed at my sweater, gripping it tight.

"Don't leave," she said again. "Come with me."

I tried to talk to the paramedics, get a little more time with the girl, but they wouldn't listen. They put her in the ambulance and hooked her up to the monitors, and she was gone. It all happened so fast.

Kathleen and I watched the sirens as they disappeared around the corner, the sound fading slowly into the night. We'd known each other for three hours, Kathleen and I. We knew we had a connection, something that bonded us together quickly—and I collapsed into her.

"You think she'll be okay?" I asked with a choked voice.

"I have to think so," she said, and the sirens were gone, the Minneapolis night once again silent and dark.

*

See, Kathleen was a recovering addict like myself. She's not afraid to share her story, and she told me everything. We had a lot in common. We had both sought to remove ourselves from reality because of the pain we were living in every single moment.

We talked until the sun came up. From that night on, we were going to be friends, and we knew it.

Kathleen was one of the first people that realized something was changing in me. She saw a light in me. Despite all the bad stuff I'd just told her about myself, about my life, about my past, she saw a future in me. She saw *me* in me. I told her about the happy coffee, and she said she was going to start her own routine with it.

About a week later, she called me on the phone. She was in tears: "Lindsey, my whole life I was a raging alcoholic. I was always chasing the feeling of being elsewhere, of being numb. I chased and chased for that next drug. And everything I've been searching for, all the peace and confidence I've never been able to find through all my traumas. . . I'm experiencing it right now in this moment. . . through a cup of coffee. I honestly cannot believe it. Thank you. Thank you so much. I am so absolutely grateful that we met."

*

Wow, right?

And Kathleen has been with me on this journey ever since. She'd also had her own financial struggles and family issues. At one point in this journey with me Kathleen was about to lose her house to tax sale. She'd had a lot of things not go her way. She needed a break. So I invited her to join my team. She did.

She had experienced, firsthand, the magic of the happy coffee and was ready to work hard and spread the word.

And you know what? Kathleen Smith was the second person on my team to go 'Diamond' with a $200,000 team of her own. In just three months, she was earning that $20,000 a month income. She saved her house. She got out of her financial abyss. She was climbing, up and up, ready to start thriving. And she did. And she is. And she's an incredible leader on my team.

And that's a little story about my friend, Kathleen.

Chapter XXVI

When One Door Closes, Another Opens

So, yeah, I mentioned earlier that when I left The Practice Company, I got 85% of my team to come with me. Big deal? I think so.

"You're pretty lucky that The Practice Company hasn't fucking sued you," a friend told me one day.

Well, maybe she shouldn't have said that one out loud either. Because a few days later, on December 31 at 9pm, New Year's Eve at 21:00, I was sued. For one-million dollars.

Fucking assholes.

They were pissed off at themselves and they were pissed off at me, and they were pissed off at the FDA, and they were pissed off at the reformulation not working—and they put their energy into coming after me. They came hard. I fought back. They lost. And then I won.

I countersued. They'd withheld my stock certificates (among other Neanderthal things in that suit), and I countersued, and I beat 'em. Those stock certificates are tucked safely away in a drawer, and only I know where they are.

I had left The Practice Company in a 100% ethical way. I did not cross recruit or reach out to any individual or entity. My team had approached me, one by one, and said, "We're coming with you."

It was like a version of *Jerry McGuire* where the sports agents really do leave the firm with Tom Cruise after he famously says, "Who's comin' with me?!" Yep, I had a whole team of Rene Zellweger's choose to leave, on their own volition, to join me and my new endeavor. I didn't even have to write a mission statement like Tom.

The Practice Company has come after me again. Come after me and my new company. But they don't have anything to go after. It's futile, but they're still doing it. I suppose I was just a good leader, a good general, and my army chose to come with me instead of sticking around for the slaughter.

Some of the suits are still technically open, so I can't really say much more than that. But, in short, I won and I felt great. Like David vs. Goliath or something.

So I'll take the millions I'm making. And I'll keep paying off the cost of all those lawsuits. And I'll keep helping people. And, The Practice Company, you can kiss my ass.

When I made the decision to leave a company whose product no longer worked so I could become part of a different entity whose product did, I had put my foot in the ground. I'd drawn a line in the sand. I didn't know if a single person on my team was going to follow me or not. Maybe one or two would, but 85%? Without even asking. That shows you something. People wanted out.

They joined me.

I wasn't even two weeks into AmpLIFEi and I had already replaced the income I'd walked away from—the instant pay, the daily pay, the monthly pay was all coming in in droves.

I texted Robert (the founder of the original formula), and was like: "Hey, I just want to say thank you for the opportunity and for believing in me and never giving up on me. I'm so glad to be here. It feels like a new home. It is a new home. Thank you."

He texted back and asked me if I still needed the cash advance I'd talked about. I said no. He said, "yeah, just imagine in a few months when you're wondering why you were ever worried about seven grand when you're making 50 grand a month."

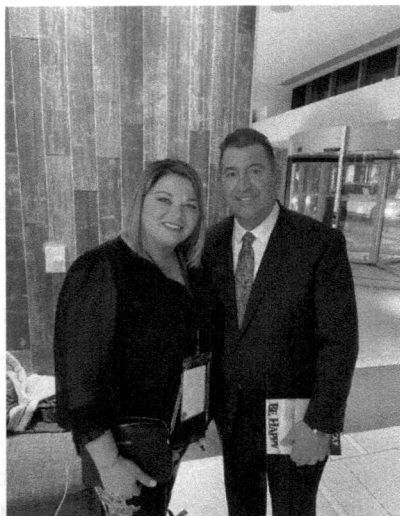

With Robert Obelon accepting my Diamond Award

Fifty-thousand dollars. As I write this sentence, that's what I'm on track for this month.

'From Fear to Fantastic.' It wasn't easy to leave my old job, my old world. But it was fantastic when I did.

Robert gave my introduction before I went up on stage to receive my Diamond Award. "Oh, Lindsey," he orated almost like something out of a roast, "it's not like you *weren't* scared. I saw that deer in headlights look in your eyes when you were making your decision to leave the other guys and come aboard over here…"

And then he spoke of my drive. Of my work ethic and my wit. And then I walked up on stage to a rousing ovation and accepted my award. It was fantastic. And there was no fear.

Chapter XXVII

Dinosaurs in the Sky

When I got together with Ryan, I cut a lot of the toxic ties in my life. He was my new family. Things were good. But there were some regrets. One main regret, really. Carrie, my best friend. When I left to go live with Ryan, I felt like I'd left her behind.

And Carrie is a butterfly, a beautiful butterfly, and she was hard to leave. She was this free, like, hippie soul. So open and free-spirited, so full of love and laughter. Yeah, she'd suffered from her share of demons, especially with addiction and depression, but she was a wonderful light.

My favorite memory of her was actually when we were cleaning a hospital together. We took our lunch break and went outside to this grassy hill to eat and get some fresh air. And I remember butterflies, butterflies like Carrie's soul, and they were all around us. Flying all around and coming to land on the grass right next to us. Our faces lit up; we were grown women, right, and it was like we were kids again. There was something so innocent about it. Butterflies all around and a couple of best friends eating our lunch under the blue sky in the green grass, clouds as white as snow. We're looking up through our 30-year-old eyes like we're ten-year-olds and finding dinosaurs in the clouds, faces and all sorts of shapes and fun things.

"Lindsey," Carrie said, "I never thought I'd find a friend like you. I never thought I'd have someone as strong or that means so much to me in my life. I never thought I'd find someone living clean in my life, what with all of my addictions."

"Oh, Carrie," I said, and I put my hand on hers.

"I never thought I'd feel free of my old behaviors. It's like we have a wide-open playground together—clean and free."

She was very proud of her sobriety. And I was very proud of her too.

*

Another day, Carrie and I were driving down a gravel road out in the country. We saw something in the road.

"Is that a dog?" I asked.

We drove closer.

"It's a pig!" Carrie said, a jubilance in her voice, again, like a child's.

We stopped the car and Carrie jumped out. Hoootin' and hollerin', she was running around trying to catch this pig! It looked like something out of a movie, some 'sister flic' or something.

I joined in. We followed that pig. It just kept running. We followed it across the prairie, passed some trees to this farm property. And the pig saunters over and walks inside this little dog-house type thing. It was the cutest thing. Carrie and I looked at each other.

"Looks like he's in the right place."

"Nicer home than a lot of the ones I grew up in!" I said, and we both laughed that laugh of innocence again.

The pig was eating from a plate of food, just like a little dog would. This wild pig, happy as could be.

Carrie and I approached him. We let him eat his food and he got comfortable with us around. We sat down in the grass next to him and rubbed his belly. I snapped a couple photos of Carrie. I still have them. I still look at them often. Shortly after these days of memory, in November of that year, I moved with Ryan. I missed Carrie immediately.

*

In June, I received a phone call. "Carrie's broken her sobriety," the voice said.

I felt like someone had punched me. I wasn't there for her.

"And she tried to kill herself," the voice went on.

I almost stopped breathing myself. I felt like I'd abandoned her.

Carrie survived her suicide attempt, but she was hospitalized. When she got out, I was the first person she called. I sat on the phone with her for hours. She talked and I listened. Then we started talking about old stories, about happy times, about butterflies and dinosaurs in the sky and pigs in the grass.

"Carrie," I said, "promise me that if you ever feel that way again that you'll call me—that I'll be the first person you call. Promise?

"I promise."

"I love you, Carrie."

"I love you too, Lindsey."

And we hung up the phone, and things were looking okay.

Until that night. I'd got a scanner a few years prior and often had it playing in the background at home at night. Just to see what was going on. Usually in the town where Ryan and I lived, but for whatever reason, that night I had it set to my hometown. The town I'd left Carrie behind in.

"Request call for ambulance and paramedics to 404 East Main Street," the scanner blared. "Adult woman, not breathing."

My heart skipped. I began to sweat. I knew that address. It was Carrie's.

Carrie had survived her first suicide attempt. She did not survive this one. I'd failed her. I should have never let her hang up the phone. When she did hang up, I should have hopped in my car and drove to her. I hadn't. I'd failed her. Carrie, my best friend, was dead.

Fuck I miss her. I miss you, Carrie.

You're my best friend.

Chapter XXVIII

Domino(s)

When we'd won the lottery, when I'd won the lottery and had Jeff in my life for those few years as a kid, things were good. It was a sepia-toned, halcyon time. It was like a good classic rock song that played on repeat for a while.

And I'd always wanted a horse.

"Can I have one, Jeff?" I asked him over and over. "Can I? Can I?"

One day he said "yes."

And that was the day that Domino came into my life. I loved him instantly. I fed him, combed him, washed him, rode him, loved him. I got my own job to pay for taking care of him. He was mine, and I loved him. My friends would come over and I'd take them to the stable and show him off. He was like this prized possession, but more so, something I could be proud of. Something I was proud of. Something I loved.

Then Jeff left. I've recounted his affair and how he left us. He was gone. And a few days later I came home from school and went out to the pasture to play with Domino. To ride him and talk to him and just be with him. He was sort of like this rock in my life, something I could count on. Feeding him apples, brushing his coat, loving him—it all gave me so much peace during those chaotic times.

He was nowhere to be found. "Domino!" I called. "Domino!"

I looked everywhere. He wasn't in the stable. He wasn't at the watering hole. He wasn't shading himself under his favorite tree. "Do-mi-no!!"

Nothing.

My mom's new boyfriend walked out of the house, slowly. He moved toward me. "I didn't want to be the one to tell you, Lindsey."

I looked at him with eyes as big as the moon.

"Your mother sold your horse."

My moon eyes began to wet. And then they flooded. The tears came fast and the tears came hard and the tears came long.

"She said she couldn't afford to keep him," he said.

That was bullshit, and I knew it. So did everyone. Sure, Jeff had bought Domino for me, but I had been working and paying, myself, to take care of him. I was paying for Domino to be in my life. I knew, as the tears kept on coming, that my mother had sold my horse to put some money in her pocket. Domino was gone, and my mom had some spending money.

It didn't seem fair. It wasn't fair. I missed Domino so very much. Still do.

Chapter XXIX

MIP (x 2)

I'd been partying from age fourteen on. I had my first beer, liked it, and kept drinking. It allowed me this feeling of escape. It allowed me to escape my mind, to get out of my head, to stop thinking about all the bad things around me and just have fun with my friends. I laughed more. I was able to really become the life of the party. It gave me more confidence with boys. I had more sex.

And, most importantly, alcohol came to give me this sense of community. Of real and big friendship. See, it was always a bunch of us doing it together—finding someone who'd buy it for us (or 'borrowing' it from our parents) and going out into a barn or the cornfields, together, for a night of fun. Alcohol helped us become closer. We'd always been close, but there was something about the disinhibition that made us even more close. More tightly knit. More sisterlike. More open and free. It was always like five, six, seven, eight, ten of us drinking our beer and being silly and getting drunk and looking at the moon and feeling happy. Feeling 'escaped.'

I came to own the role of 'the life of the party.' I loved the attention, sought it out, was never afraid to make a fool out of myself just to make someone laugh. The laughter was a big part of it. I hadn't had a ton of laughter in my life up to that point. And laughing, and seeing my friends laughing, and laughing all together felt good. Alcohol felt good. I liked it.

I drank all through high school, whenever I could. I started drinking a lot.

Then, as a freshman in college, something really cool happened. There was this annual party, The Barn Party,

140

and it was pretty rare for a freshman to get invited. I got the invite. I felt cool. I got dressed up and we piled in my car and we drove out to place.

Everyone was there. It was a big ol' shindig. The kegs were flowing and the talk was rambunctious, the laughter loud and good and free. I felt an acceptance I had always yearned for. My peers liked me. I'd been invited and I was making people laugh. All was good. Until it wasn't.

We saw the blue and red sirens through the window.

"It's the cops!" came the muffled shouts. "Fuck!"

They locked us in the barn. It was almost like something out of the film *Braveheart*. They literally locked us in the barn, and though it wasn't burning down it felt like it. The laughter became a heavy silence. They started pulling us out one-by-one. They put those over 21 in one line and those of us under 21 in another. Those of us in my line all got MIPs. It wasn't fun.

But, like the college kid I was, I brushed it off as 'all part of the experience' and the very next weekend I was back at the kegger. A fun little house party and the laughter was loud again. I was escaped and feeling free. Then, well then, the sirens came again. I got my second MIP in two weeks.

I was forced to go to AA. Walking in those doors was eye opening for me. Hearing all the stories from around the circle of chairs. All the "Hello, my name is ____, and I'm an alcoholic." It hit home.

I went into Doctor Staley's office, a professor at my school and a man I trusted very much. A man I looked up to. A man I listened to.

"Wow, Lindsey," he said. "Two weekends in a row. That's impressive."

"Do you think I have a problem?"

"I don't know. Could be bad luck, could be something more. Let's try this. . ."

He told me to make a commitment to not drink for 30 days. To make a firm commitment not to drink for a month, and if I could do it then I probably didn't have a problem—but if I made the commitment and went to a party or something and was overcome to drink, then it was something I needed to look seriously at.

I made the commitment to myself. I didn't want to end up like my mom or the other alcoholics in my family. I got my schoolwork done and did go to parties where there was alcohol. People offered me beers and I declined.

I was still able to make people laugh. Still able to be the life of the party. I knew, at that point, that I did not *need* alcohol. It never became an addiction like food did.

To this day, I still drink socially. And I enjoy it. But I keep an eye on it, never allowing it to take control over my life.

With alcohol in my system, yeah, I've made some mistakes. Slept with some men I shouldn't have. Fought a girl once, and I regretted it. But by-and-large, I've been able to control my drinking and use it for its intended purpose. I know the history of alcoholism in my family and so I keep a vigilant eye on my drinking.

And if any of you reading this book ever see me start to drink too much or too regularly, see me get out of hand, let me know. I'll do the same for you. We don't need alcohol or drugs or codependency. For me, all I need is coffee. It may be all that you need too.

142

Chapter XXX

Help, It's What I do.

I can honestly say that I know I have made an impact on hundreds of people's lives. That feels good. (That number may even be in the thousands.) And that is what we are put here on this planet to do; we humans are social creatures, social animals, and it is through the group that we have come to be a great species. It is through working together, through helping thy neighbor and lifting people up.

I was not dealt the best hand in life. I did not have the most stable childhood. Bad shit has happened to me. I've had to work to make myself happy. And a lot of that has been through making other people happy. Through making other people healthier. Through helping people, and the world, thrive.

And while you can go to my Facebook and read what my team says about the type of leader I am and you can go to peruse the hundreds of testimonials about what I have done for them, I always want to keep doing *more*. More help. More inspiration. More triumph. That is what the world needs. These last couple years have been tough, what with Covid and all that, and life was hard enough before. Making life better—that's my game.

And giving speeches, talking in front of humans, is one way that I achieve that. Maybe it was some intuition from back when I was in high school speech class. I remember the assignment; we had to "give a speech and we present it in a unique way." Well, as a teenager, with all that I had been through, yep, I gave that speech on suicide. The whole thing. They whos, whats, whys, and hows. That's where my mind was at. That's where my soul was at. And at that age, I didn't even see it, didn't see how fucked up that was. It took a long time for me on my journey to stop speaking about suicide and start speaking on inspiration. All of us have to go through a certain metamorphosis in our life—like the butterfly on the other side of the caterpillar's cocoon.

For me, I just want people to see the positive in things. I want people to live positively and happily. To get the best out of our time on this planet.

That's why when I speak in front of crowds, now, I go with ultimate positivity. I tell my story not so people can feel sorry for what I have had to endure but rather so people can find the inspiration to overcome the difficult things in their life.

Back in my 20s, I got into this thing called 'The Diversion Program.' It was a way to keep kids out of trouble, and I was speaking to crowds all across Nebraska. And I connected with people. I lifted them up.

That Christmas, I got a card from a mom and her daughter, both of whom had been to hear me speak.

"Lindsey," the mother wrote, "You saved my daughter's life. She told me that if I hadn't dragged her there to see you speak, she had the intention of killing herself that very night. What you said struck a chord in her. What you said made her want to *live*."

Reading that letter was one of the moments that makes it all worth it. Yeah, everyone wants to make a lot of money, but it is the impact we have on a personal level with other human beings that makes the world go round.

More letters came. All super positive, all about how people's lives were different, better, after hearing what I had to say up on stage. I've saved them. Helped to at least.

And these letters, I get them out every once in a while and read them. Reread them—just to remind myself of the mission I am on. It's part of my process, because, by nature, I am a pretty darn humble person, and I have to remind myself that I am doing good. Have to remind myself that I am doing awesome. That I am living the flow and helping people.

I don't know if I was born like this or my life has drilled it into me, but because of my natural humility, I do have to sometimes stop, take a step back, and say, "Wow, Lindsey, you're doing good work. You *are* helping. You're making your impact."

We all have to do that sometimes. We get so caught up in the day-to-day and we can be so hard on ourselves. Way harder on ourselves than other people are on us. That's something I talk about a lot. Giving yourself credit—if you're doing the work, give yourself the credit you deserve. You've earned it.

So, dear reader, give yourself credit. And do good. Believe in yourself and help people. You can make the world a better place. You can make your life beautiful. You can be fulfilled. You can be happy. Truly happy.

Chapter the Last

New Beginnings

What more could a girl want!!

My life is flourishing. My business is nearing a million dollars a month in sales. My marriage and my relationship with my husband are stronger than they have ever been. My stepson Reid is with us full time and Jayden is excelling in school and athletics. Jhetta, amid all the drama that is Junior High, is learning tons and finding her way— and late in 2020, she asked Ryan to adopt her so she could officially become a Buboltz. Her wish came true. So has mine: I am traveling the world and living the dream.

But, as my story has gone, this is just about when the bottom is about to drop. Right? Well, it did.

I was headed to Pigeon Forge, Tennessee for a week-long retreat with 62 other women amongst the grandeur of the Smoky Mountains. I had been asked to head a training session, and I was jazzed—my life's work was about to be showcased amongst a woman's biggest critics: other women.

I'd held out writing the final chapter of this book because none other than Oprah was scheduled to share the stage with me. Oprah! Are you kidding me? It was my time to shine. It was time to show the world that I was made for more—and that I deserved to be *on*—the stage.

But then Ms. Winfrey scratched. Whatever, I'm sure she has a busy schedule and all. And what transpired during the retreat turned out to be way more impactful than any celebrity speech. Way more profound, in fact, than any of us could have ever imagined.

*

I'm leading my training session. Up on stage and engaging my people—my downlines, my uplines, my sidelines—and I'm in my element. I'm firing on all cylinders. I'm speaking and teaching and leading. Things couldn't be going more smoothly.

Then the front door burst open. There are shouts. "Stop!" I hear. "Stop!!" I look up. It was Laura, my dear friend and President of AmpLIFEi. She had a look of panic and desperation in her eye.

The room went silent and I ran to her as tears streamed down her face. She could barely speak. "Go!" she said to me finally. "Go—go... there's been an accident, her little girl..."

"Wh—whose little girl?" I asked, fear thick on my tongue.

I ran through the mansion-cabin that was our retreat center in a blur, not knowing which one of us was losing their daughter. I was just running around looking for a mother, *the* mother, the entire time praying to the Lord, "Please don't let it be one of my girls." I didn't know if I could take more losses.

I ran up the first flight of stairs—then I was stopped in my tracks by the deafening sound of a suitcase thudding down the steps. I rounded the corner and saw the suitcase and then the woman to whom it belonged: my teammate, my personally-enrolled, my dear friend. I saw the look in her eye that I knew too well: Absolute terror. Absolute despair. She was the mother I had been unconsciously searching for. She was the woman who needed me—because back in the Midwest her eight-year-old daughter, Hope, was succumbing to injuries sustained from a farming accident. And Hope would not make it.

I knew what my friend was going through. I saw it in an instant. I recognized it. The pure hell.

What I didn't know was if I would have the strength to be the friend I needed to be in her hour of need.

I spent ten hours garnering the strength to do what needed to be done. To confront my past and be there for this woman who needed me. I walked up to her. I held her. I hugged her. And then I spoke the most honest words ever to leave my mouth:

"It's going to suck," I told her. "It's going to hurt. It's going to test every ounce of everything in you." She was looking in my eyes. She was listening, and so I kept speaking. "This will test your mind," I said, "test your relationships. It will test your marriage. I can't tell you that it's 'going to be okay,' but what I can tell you, having lived through what you are now living through, is that *you*—you can make it through."

And I held my friend and absorbed her tears, all the memory of Shakiah's death flooding within me.

*

Hope will not be just a memory. Hope, like her namesake, will be a Legacy. Because she will live on through her death, live on through the lives of her mother and father, live on as the story of her life impacts the world. She already has.

That impact began the very next day after her death. Eleven of us women came forward to be baptized. Myself included. We had been so touched, so moved by everything that we'd experienced that we came forward for the Healing. Hope's life had moved each of us closer to God.

148

Her Legacy had begun. She was inspiring us. She was awing us. Indescribable events came to transpire. God was everywhere. Healing, for everybody, for all of us, came in waves. Because of Hope.

Old hurt would resurface, we knew, but the story of Survival would prevail.

And I came to discover that it wasn't coffee that saved my life after all—it was God, it was the Universe, it was Jesus and the sense of purpose that came over me to share my story. To share all that life has dealt me. To share all that you have just read.

My life, my story.

Because somewhere in this world there is another child. Another mother. Another wife. Another sister or niece or friend who needs to know they are not alone—who needs to know that after the darkness, there is always Light.

PIERUCCI PUBLISHING

We're Publishing!

Are you a mindful author, entrepreneur, coach, or healer looking to contribute your wisdom to the current world awakening?

Pierucci Publishing is committed to publishing mindful authors and experts committed to elevating the world through books and impactful stories.

Are you one of them?

Please find us at www.PierucciPublishing.com to apply.

About The Author

Have you ever hit rock bottom? You're not alone. Lindsey Buboltz, mother, wife, successful entrepreneur, speaker, and coach, finally shares the story behind her success... and it's not what you'd think.

Far from growing up with a silver spoon, Lindsey tells the tale of abandonment by her parents, abuse, and even a murder that almost caused her to end her own life for good. And then one day Lindsey woke up with a *jolt*.

It was the day after a near suicide attempt; Lindsey didn't know if she could make it out of bed. But somebody handed her a very special elixir that changed her life for good. Lindsey has lifted herself out of enough pain and tragedy to fill 100 lifetimes.

In *Coffee Saved My Life*, Lindsey is going to tell you how she went from brokenhearted and destitute to building a million dollar business almost overnight. You won't believe your eyes.

(And, yeah... grab a tissue... make it the whole box!)

Lindsey has been featured on:

> Leaving Nothing to Chance Podcast w/ John Solledar
>
> Scott Schilling Speaks Podcast w/ Scott Schilling Network Marketing Times, Feature Article, Mar 16, 2021
>
> Speaker- Les Brown Hope Tour 2019
>
> Keynote Speaker- Amplified Women's Retreat 2021
>
> Business for Home Feature 2019
>
> Business for Home Feature 2021
>
> Elevate: Elevating Entrepreneurship, 3rd Edition Volume 1: Cover and Featured Article

Share the Love

Join the party by scanning this code or heading to LindseyBuboltz.com where you can find the latest information about Lindsey, her magical coffee, and her prosperous team!

Are you our next Coffee Millionaire?

Gratitude Space

Notes